丛书主编　彭新良

The Double Ninth Festival

汉英对照

重阳节

李晓燕　谢黎蕾　编著

曾静　译

全国百佳图书出版单位

APTIME
时代出版

时代出版传媒股份有限公司

安徽人民出版社

图书在版编目（CIP）数据

重阳节：汉英对照 / 李晓燕，谢黎蕾编著；曾静译. -- 合肥：安徽人民出版社，2018.8
（多彩中国节丛书 / 彭新良主编）

ISBN 978-7-212-10029-2

Ⅰ. ①重… Ⅱ. ①李… ②谢… ③曾… Ⅲ. ①节日－风俗习惯－中国－汉、英 Ⅳ. ① K892.1

中国版本图书馆 CIP 数据核字 (2018) 第 005209 号

《多彩中国节》丛书

重阳节：汉英对照
CHONGYANG JIE

彭新良　丛书主编
李晓燕　谢黎蕾　编著　　曾静　译

出 版 人：徐　敏　　　　　　选题策划：刘　哲　陈　娟
出版统筹：张　旻　袁小燕　　责任编辑：周冰倩
责任印制：董　亮　　　　　　装帧设计：陈　爽　宋文岚

出版发行：时代出版传媒股份有限公司 http://www.press-mart.com
　　　　　安徽人民出版社 http://www.ahpeople.com
地　　址：合肥市政务文化新区翡翠路 1118 号出版传媒广场八楼
邮　　编：230071
电　　话：0551-63533258　0551-63533259（传真）
印　　刷：安徽联众印刷有限公司

开本：880mm×1230mm　1/32　印张：6.75　字数：200 千
版次：2018 年 8 月第 1 版　　2018 年 9 月第 1 次印刷

ISBN　978-7-212-10029-2　　　　　　定价：35.00 元

代 序

我们共同的日子

个人一年一度最重要的日子是生日,大家一年一度最重要的日子是节日。节日是大家共同的日子。

节日是一种纪念日,内涵多种多样。有民族的、国家的、宗教的,比如国庆节、圣诞节等。有某一类人的,如妇女、儿童、劳动者的,这便是妇女节、儿童节、劳动节等。也有与人们的生活生产密切相关的,这类节日历史悠久,很早就形成了一整套人们约定俗成、代代相传的节日习俗,这是一种传统的节日。传统节日也多种多样。中国是一个多民族国家,有 56 个民族,统称中华民族。传统节日有全民族共有的,也有某个民族特有的。比如春节、中秋节、元宵节、端午节、清明节、重阳节等,就为中华民族所共用和共享;世界文化遗产羌年就为羌族独有和独享。各民族这样的节日很多。

传统节日是在漫长的农耕时代形成的。农耕时代生产与生活、人与自然的关系十分密切。人们或为了感恩于大自然的恩赐,或为了庆祝辛勤劳作换来的收获,或为了激发生命的活力,或为了加强人际的亲情,经过长期相互认同,最终约定俗成,渐渐把一年中某一天确定为节日,并创造了十分完整又严格的节俗,如仪式、庆典、规制、禁忌,乃至特定的游艺、装饰与食品,来把节日这天演化成一个独具内涵、迷人的日子。更重要的是,人们在每一个传统的节日里,还把共同的生活理想、人间愿望与审美追求融入节日的内涵与种种仪式中。因此,它是中华民族世间理想与生活愿望极致的表现。可以说,我们的传统——精神文化传统,往往就是依靠这代代相传的一年一度的节日继承下来的。

然而,自从 20 世纪整个人类进入由农耕文明向工业文明的过渡,农耕时代形成的文化传统开始瓦解。尤其是中国,在近百年由封闭走向开放的过程中,节日文化——特别是城市的节日文化受到现代文明与外来文化的冲击。当下人们已经鲜明地感受到传统节日渐行渐远,并为此产生忧虑。传统节日的淡化必然使其中蕴含的传统精神随之涣散。然而,人们并没有坐等传统的消失,主动和积极地与之应对。这充分显示了当代中国人在文化上的自觉。

近 10 年,随着中国民间文化遗产抢救工程的全面展开,国家非物质文化遗产名录申报工作的有力推动,传统节日受到关注,一些重要的传统节日被列入了国家文化遗产名录。继而,2006 年国家将每年 6 月的第二个周六确定为"文化遗产日",2007 年国务院决定将 3 个中华民族的重要节日——清明节、端午节和中秋节列为法定放假日。这一重大决定,表现了国家对公众的传统文化生活及其传承的重视与尊重,同时也是保护节日文化遗产十分必要的措施。

节日不放假必然直接消解了节日文化,放假则是恢复节日传统的首要条件。但放假不等于远去的节日立即就会回到身边。节日与假日的不同是因为节日有特定的文化内容与文化形式。那么,重温与恢复已经变得陌生的传统节日习俗则是必不可少的了。

千百年来,我们的祖先从生活的愿望出发,为每一个节日都创造出许许多多美丽又动人的习俗。这种愿望是理想主义的，所以节日习俗是理想的；愿望是情感化的，所以节日习俗也是情感化的；愿望是美好的，所以节日习俗是美的。人们用合家团聚的年夜饭迎接新年；把天上的明月化为手中甜甜的月饼，来象征人间的团圆；在严寒刚刚消退、万物复苏的早春，赶到野外去打扫墓地，告慰亡灵，表达心中的缅怀，同时戴花插柳，踏青春游，亲切地拥抱大地山川……这些诗意化的节日习俗，使我们一代代人的心灵获得了美好的安慰与宁静。

对于少数民族来说，他们特有的节日的意义则更加重要。节日还是他们民族集体记忆的载体、共同精神的依托、个性的表现、民族身份之所在。

谁说传统的习俗过时了？如果我们淡忘了这些习俗，就一定要去重温一下传统。重温不是表象地模仿古人的形式，而是用心去体验传统中的精神与情感。

在历史进程中，习俗是在不断变化的，但民族传统的精神实质不应变。这传统就是对美好生活的不懈追求，对大自然的感恩与敬畏，对家庭团圆与世间和谐永恒的企望。

这便是我们节日的主题，也是这套《多彩中国节》丛书编写的根由与目的。

中国 56 个民族是一个大家庭，各民族的节日文化异彩纷呈，既有春节、元宵节、中秋节这样多民族共庆的节日，也有泼水节、火把节、那达慕等少数民族特有的节日。这套丛书选取了中国最有代表性的 10 个传统节日，一节一册，图文并茂，汉英对照，旨在为海内外读者通俗、全面地呈现中国绚丽多彩的节庆文化和民俗文化；放在一起则是中华民族传统节日的一部全书，既有知识性、资料性、工具性，又有可读性和趣味性。10 本精致的小册子，以翔实的文献和生动的传说，将每个节日的源起、流布与习俗，图文并茂、有滋有味地娓娓道来，从这些节日的传统中，可以看出中国人的精神追求和文化脉络。这样一套丛书不仅是对我国传统节日的一次总结，也是对传统节日文化富于创意的弘扬。

我读了书稿，心生欣喜，因序之。

冯骥才

（全国政协常委、中国文联原执行副主席）

Preface

Our Common Days

The most important day for a person is his or her birthday while the most important days for all are festivals, which are our common days.

Festivals are embedded with rich connotations for remembering. There're ethnic, national, and religious ones, such as National Day and Christmas Day; festivals for a certain group of people, such as Women's Day, Children's Day, and Laborers' Day; and those closely related to people's life and production, which enjoy a long history and feature a complete set of well-established festive traditions passed on from one generation to another. These are so-called traditional festivals, which vary greatly, too.

China, consisting of 56 nationalities, is a multi-ethnic country. People in China are collectively called the Chinese nation. So it's no wonder that some of the traditional festivals are celebrated by all nationalities while others only by certain nationalities, with the representatives of the former ones being the Spring Festival, the Lantern Festival, the Dragon Boat Festival, the Tomb-Sweeping Festival, and the Double Ninth Festival, etc. and that of the latter being the Qiang New Year, a unique festival for Qiang ethnic group. Each of ethnic groups in China has quite a number of their unique traditional festivals.

The traditional festivals have taken shape in the long agrarian times when people were greatly dependent on nature and when life was closely related to production. People gradually saw eye to eye with each other in the long-term practicing sets of rituals, celebrations, taboos as well as games, embellishments, and foods in a strict way and decided to select some days of one year as festivals with a view to expressing their gratitude to nature, celebrating harvesting, stimulating vitality of life, or strengthening bonds between family members and relatives. In this way, festivals have evolved into charming days with unique connotations. More importantly, people have instilled their common aspirations and aesthetic pursuits into festive connotations and rituals. To put it simply, festivals are consummate demonstrations of Chinese people's worldly aspirations and ideals, and Chinese people's spiritual cultures are inherited for generations by them.

Nevertheless, the cultural traditions formed in the agrarian times began to collapse with human beings being in transition from agrarian civilization to industrial one, esp., in China, whose festive cultures were severely hammered by modern civilization and foreign cultures in nearly one hundred years from being closed to opening up to the world. Nowadays, people strongly feel that traditional festivals are drifting away from their lives and are deeply concerned about it owing to the fact that dilution of traditional festivals means the fall of the traditional spirit of Chinese people. Of course, we don't wait and see; instead, we cope with it in a positive way. This fully displays the contemporary Chinese people's cultural consciousness.

In recent ten years, the traditional festivals have been earning more and more attention and some significant ones are included to the list of the National Heritages with the vigorous promotion of China's Folk Heritage Rescue Program and China's intangible cultural heritage application; for example, China set the second Saturday of June as "Cultural Heritage Day" in 2006; the State Council decided to list three significant traditional festivals as legal holidays—the Tomb-Sweeping Festival, the Dragon Boat Festival, and the Mid-Autumn Festival in 2007. These measures show the state gives priority to and pay tribute to the inheritance of public traditional cultures.

Holidays are necessary for spending festivals which will be diluted otherwise; however, holidays don't necessarily bring back traditional festivals. Since festivals, different from holidays, are equipped with special cultural forms and contents, it's essential to recover those traditional festive customs which have become stranger and stranger to contemporary Chinese people.

In the past thousands of years, our ancestors, starting from their aspirations, created many fine and engaging traditions. These aspirations are ideal, emotional, and beautiful, so are the festival traditions. People usher in the New Year by having the meal together on the New Year's Eve, make moon cakes by imitating the moon in the sky, standing for family reunion, or go to sweep the tombs of ancestors or family members for commemorating or comforting in the early spring when the winter just recedes and everything wakes up while taking spring hiking and enjoying spring scenes by the way. These poetic festive customs greatly comfort souls of people for generations.

As for ethnic minority people, their special festivals mean more to them. The festivals carry the collective memory, common spirit, character of their ethnic groups as well as mark their ethnic identities.

Are the traditional festive customs really out-dated? We're compelled to review them if we really forget them. What matters for review is not imitating the forms of the ancient Chinese people's celebrations but experiencing essence and emotions embedded in them with heart and soul.

Traditions have evolved with history's evolving, but the traditional national spirit has never changed. The spirit lies in people's never-ending pursuit for beautiful life, consistent gratitude and awe for nature, constant aspiration for family reunion and world harmony.

This is also the theme of our festivals and the root-cause of compiling the series.

The Chinese nation, featuring its colorful and varieties of festive cultures, boasts the common festivals celebrated by all nationalities, such as the Spring Festival, the Lantern Festival, the Mid-Autumn Festival, and the ethnic festivals, such as the Water Splashing Festival (Thai people), the Torch Festival (Yi people), Naadam (Mongolian nationality). This series, selecting the most typical ten festivals of China, with each festival being in one volume with figures and in both English and Chinese, unfolds the colorful festive and folk cultures in an engaging and all-round way for appealing to foreign readers. If put together, they constitute a complete set of books on Chinese traditional festivals, being instructive and intriguing. The ten brochures elaborate on the origins, distribution, and customs of each festival in an engaging way with figures, tales, and rich literature. Chinese people's spiritual pursuit and cultural veining can be tracked in this series, serving as a summary of Chinese traditional festivals and innovative promotion of them.

I went over the series with delight, and with delight, wrote the preface, too.

Feng Jicai

CPPCC National Committee member

Former Vice-president of the China Federation of Literary and Art Circles

目 录

第一章 重阳节的起源与传承

一、重阳节的起源……………………… 002

二、重阳节的传承……………………… 010

第二章 重阳节的习俗

一、重阳节食俗………………………… 036

二、重阳节佩俗………………………… 044

三、重阳节民俗………………………… 047

第三章 重阳节的特色节庆地

一、泰山登山节………………………… 106

二、江西秋社节………………………… 110

三、开封菊花会………………………… 113

四、铜陵龙烛会………………………… 118

五、潮汕菊花宴………………………… 120

第四章　少数民族地区和港澳台的重阳节

一、少数民族的重阳节·····················148

二、港澳台地区的重阳节·················157

第五章　重阳节的海外传播

一、韩国重阳节·····························178

二、日本重阳节·····························179

附录："菊花酒"的酿制方法······188

丛书后记·····························191

多彩中国节

重阳节

Contents

Chapter One

The Origin and Inheritance of the Double Ninth Festival

1. The Origin of the Double Ninth Festival / 017

2. The Inheritance of the Double Ninth Festival / 026

Chapter Two

The Traditions of the Double Ninth Festival

1. The Food Customs of the Double Ninth Festival / 066

2. The Wearing Traditions of the Double Ninth Festival / 076

3. The Folk Customs of the Double Ninth Festival / 082

Chapter Three

The Special Local Celebrations of The Double Ninth Festival

1. Mount Tai International Mountaineering Festival / 125

2. The Autumn Sacrifice Festival of Jiangxi Province / 129

3. The Kaifeng Chrysanthemum Fair / 132

4. The Tongling Dragon Candle Fair / 139

5. The Chrysanthemum Banquet of Chaozhou and Shantou in Guangdong Province / 141

Chapter Four

The Double Ninth Festival in Ethnic Minority Regions & in Hong Kong, Macao, and Taiwan

1. The Double Ninth Festival in Ethic Minority Regions / 161

2. The Double Ninth Festival in Horg Kong,Macao,and Taiwan / 172

Chapter Five

The Overseas Communication of the Double Ninth Festival

1. The Double Ninth Festival in South Korea / 183

2. The Double Ninth Festival in Japan / 184

Appendix:Recipe of Brewing Chrysanthemam wine

Series Postscript / 183

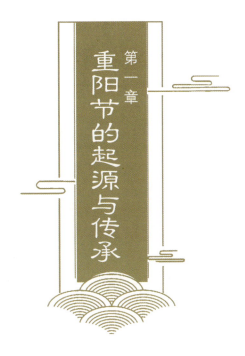

第一章 重阳节的起源与传承

　　每年的农历九月初九，是中国的传统节日——重阳节。
重阳节又称"登高节""茱萸节""老人节""女儿节"。
这一天，人们有登高、赏菊、饮菊花酒、插茱萸、吃重阳糕、
放风筝的习俗。"重阳"一词有何意义？这些别称从何而来？
重阳节在中国的历史长河中又经历了怎样的发展呢？

一、重阳节的起源

　　农历九月初九，是中国传统的重阳节。在中国古人的哲学观里，将天地万物归为阴阳两级，阴代表黑暗，阳代表光明。数字也不例外。古人把数字也分为阴数和阳数，具体来说就是偶数为阴，奇数为阳。九为奇数，因此属阳，九月初九，日月都为九，二阳相重，所以称"九月初九"为"重阳"，也叫"重九"。据考证，重阳节始于远古，形成于春秋战国，普及于西汉，鼎盛于唐朝。重阳又称"踏秋"，与农历三月三的"踏青"相似，都是全家扶老携幼，倾室而出，一起出游赏景、登高望远。因而，重阳节又名登高节、菊花节、茱萸节、老人节、女儿节等。

　　由于农历九月初九中的"九九"与"久久"同音，而九在数字中又是最大数，所以也赋予了重阳节长久、长寿的含义。人们经常在这一天祭祀祖先，推行敬老活动。重阳节与除夕、清明、中元三节并称中国祭祀的四大节日。

　　关于重阳节起源的说法，由于年代久远，所以节日的起源和形成的过程不易考察。关于如今的重阳节有许多不同的说法。

（一）上古九月的庆典

对于农耕社会来说，农历九月农事已经基本完毕。由于食物充足，且大家有了休息时间，所以从远古时期，华夏先民就把丰年的庆典和祭祀仪式安排在了农历九月。

《吕氏春秋·季秋纪》中记载，到了农历九月农作物丰收的时候，先民们举行祭祀天地和祖先等岁时活动，到了战国时期，这一习俗被统治者加以条令化和典章化。

由于是庆祝丰收年的活动，所以农历九月的丰收庆典带有娱乐和狂欢的色彩，庆典伴随有很多娱乐内容，比如饮酒、野餐、歌舞等。后人普遍认为，汉代以后，重阳节的野宴、饮酒、歌舞等习俗，是源于先秦的农历九月庆典。所以，有人把先秦农历的九月盛典也称为是"酒神节"。这大概是重阳节最早的雏形。

（二）先秦的火神崇拜

重阳节的原型之一是古代的祭祀大火的仪式。在原始社会，人们非常崇拜能够带来光和热的火。

先民把天空中一颗亮度很高的恒星叫作"心宿二星"，并把"心宿二星"看作是火神的化身，称它为"大火"。人们通过观察大火星出没的位置，来确定季节的转换。

由于大火星具有划分季节的作用，传说在4000多年前，中国上古时代的首领颛顼，专门设立了一个官职来负责观测这颗恒星。到了农历九月，这颗作为季节标志的恒星隐退，意味着冬季逐渐来临。由于原始先民抵御寒冷的能力有限，加上食物很难维持一整个冬季，许多人会在寒冷中死去。先民认为，带来光和热的火神暂时隐退，妖魔鬼怪趁此机会横行人间，很多人即将死亡。因此，先民会在农历九月举办各种仪式来祭祀火神，祈求平安。古人到底怎么样来祭祀火神呢？我们现代人已经很难知晓了，但我们还是可以从现在还存在的一些重阳节仪式中寻找到一些古俗遗痕。比如，江南部分地区有重阳节祭灶的习俗，其中祭祀的对象就是家家户户厨房里掌管灶火的灶神，这应该是古代农历九月祭祀大火的遗俗之一吧。

先秦这种对火的崇拜，成为后来重阳节求长寿、消灾避邪等习俗的重要来源。而农历九月初九的祭祀活动，成为我国社会农耕文明的重要组成部分。

○厨房供奉的灶王爷画像

祭　灶　神

祭灶神是一项在中国民间影响很大、流传极广的传统习俗。很多家庭灶间都设有"灶王爷"神位。人们称这尊神为"司命菩萨"或"灶君司命"，传说他是掌管人间的玉皇大帝封的灶王，负责管理各家的灶火，被作为各家的保护神而受到崇拜。灶王龛大都设在灶房的北面或东面，中间供上灶王爷的神像。没有灶王龛的人家，也有将神像直接贴在墙上的。有的神像只画灶王爷一人，有的则有男女两人，女神被称为"灶王奶奶"。灶神是中国民间最富代表性，最有广泛群众基础的流行神之一，寄托了中国劳动人民一种辟邪除灾、迎祥纳福的美好愿望。农历十二月二十三日或二十四日为中国传统的祭灶日。但在江南一些地区也有九月初九重阳节这一天祭灶的习俗。

（三）神话传说

由于年代久远，重阳节的形成很难有确切的考证，但和我国的其他一些传统节日一样，重阳节的由来也与一些神话传说密不可分。

1. 桓景斗瘟魔

南朝吴均所作的志怪小说集《续齐谐记》中记载着这样一个故事：东汉时期，河南汝南县有个人名叫桓景。他和父母妻子一家人守着几块地，安分守己地过日子。谁知天有不测风云，汝河两岸忽然流行起瘟疫，夺走了不少人的性命。桓景小时候曾听大人说过，汝河里住了一个瘟魔，每年都会出来散布瘟疫，为害人间。为了替乡民除害，桓景打听到东南山中住了一个叫费长房的神仙，就决定前去拜访。

谁知他翻越了千山万水，还是找不到仙人的踪迹。有一天，他忽然看见面前站着一只雪白的鸽子不断地向他点头，桓景走近前一看，鸽子忽然飞了两三丈远，落地后又不断地向桓景点头。就这样，桓景跟着白鸽，终于找到了费长房的仙居。桓景走到门口，恭恭敬敬地跪了两天两夜。到了第三天，大门忽然开了，一位白发老人笑眯眯地对他说："弟子为民除害心切，快跟我进院吧！"

费长房给了桓景一把降妖青龙剑，让他练习降妖的法门。有一天桓景正在练剑，费长房走过来对他说："今年九月九，汝河瘟魔又要出来害人。你赶紧回乡为民除害，我给你茱萸叶子一包，菊花酒一瓶，让你家乡父老登高避祸。"说完，就用手招来一只仙鹤，把桓景载回汝南去了。

桓景回到家乡，就把费长房的话向大伙儿说了一遍。到了九月九那天，他就带着全村老少登上了附近的一座山。桓景避灾所登的这座山冈，春秋时名冈山（今日上蔡的芦冈）。冈山南北长25千米，东西宽7千米，高97.2千米，上土下石。上蔡境内唯此山最高，登上冈陵，可以眺望田野。

桓景把茱萸叶子分给每人一片，让瘟魔不敢近前。又把菊花酒倒出来，每人喝了一口，说是可以避瘟疫。安排妥当后，他就带着降妖青龙剑回到村中，等着斩杀瘟魔。

不一会儿，汝河上狂风怒吼，瘟魔出水走上岸来。抬头看见人群都在山上欢聚，它便冲至山下，却被酒气及茱萸的香味吓得不敢上前。一回头，又看见桓景抽出宝剑。桓景和瘟魔斗了几个回合，瘟魔斗他不过，转身就跑。桓景"嗖"的一声掷出了宝剑，宝剑闪着寒光，一眨眼就把瘟魔钉死在地上。

从此汝河两岸的百姓，再也不受瘟疫的侵袭了。人们就把九月九日登高避祸、插茱萸、喝菊花酒的习俗，一代代地传到今天。

○漫画"桓景除瘟魔"

而传说中的汝南正是现在河南省的上蔡县。上蔡县被称为我国重阳节的起源地。2003年国家邮政局在上蔡县举办了重阳节特种邮票首发仪式。2005年12月，上蔡县被正式命名为"中国重阳文化之乡"，成为目前国内唯一以传统节日命名的文化之乡。2006年3月，上蔡县重阳习俗被河南省人民政府收入第一批省级非物质文化遗产保护名录，2011年6月，被国务院批准列入第三批国家级非物质文化遗产。上蔡不仅历史悠久，人才辈出，境内名胜古迹众多，而且还是古代文明和民族传统文化的聚集地和发祥地之一，蕴涵了丰富的历史文化。传说在远古时期，人类的始祖羲氏在此观物取象画出了反映中国古代哲学思想的"八卦图"。之后教人结网狩猎、驯养家畜、开物成务，后人感其恩德，在蔡河建伏羲祠以示纪念。上蔡县还是古蔡国所在地，距今已有3000多年的文明历史。

○2003年国家邮政局发行的"九九重阳节"特种邮票，内容分别是"登高""赏菊""饮酒对弈"

2. 骊山传说

传说在很早以前，有个庄户人家住在骊山下，全家人都很勤快，日子过得也不错。

有一天，这家主人从地里回来，半路上碰到个算卦先生。眼看天快黑了，这先生还没找到歇处。由于主人家里很窄，只有个草棚子，于是主人就在灶房里打了个草铺，让妻子儿女都在草铺上睡，自己陪着算卦先生睡在炕上，凑合着住。

第二天天刚亮，算卦先生要走。庄户人叫醒妻子给先生做了一顿好吃喝，又给先生装了一袋白蒸馍。算卦先生出了门，看了看庄户人住的地方，叮咛他说："到九月九，全家高处走。"庄户人想，我平日没做啥坏事，又不想升官，上高处走啥呢？但又一想，人常说算命先生会看风水，精通天文，说不定我住的地方会出啥麻烦。到了九月九，就到高处走一走吧，就当让全家人看看风景。

到了九月九，庄户人就带着妻子儿女背上花糕香酒，登上骊山高峰去游玩。等他们上山后，半山腰突然冒出一股泉水直冲他家，把他家的草棚子一下子就冲垮了。不大功夫，整个一条山沟都被淹了。庄户人家这才明白算卦先生为什么让他全家九月九登高。

这事传开后，人们就每逢农历九月九，扶老携幼去登高，相沿成俗，一直流传至今。

○骊山风光

旅游小贴士

骊　山

骊山是中国古今驰名的风景游览胜地，位于陕西省西安市临潼县城南，距离西安市区 30 多千米。骊山是秦岭山脉的一个支脉，东西绵亘 25 千米，南北宽约 13.7 千米，海拔 1302 米，山上松柏长青，壮丽翠秀，因外形似一匹青苍的骊驹而得名。它是华清宫景区的重要组成部分，是著名的道教名山，山上文物古迹众多、自然景观秀丽。从周、秦、汉、唐以来，这里一直作为皇家园林地，离宫别墅众多。

地址：西安市临潼区环城东路 3 号

二、
重阳节的传承

重阳节，早在战国时期就已经形成，到了唐代被正式定为民间的节日，此后历朝历代沿袭至今。重阳与三月初三"踏春"都是家族倾室而出的节日。庆祝重阳节一般包括出游赏秋、登高远眺、观赏菊花、遍插茱萸、吃重阳糕、饮菊花酒等活动。

（一）重阳节的起源时期

重阳的源头，可追溯到先秦之前。秦国丞相吕不韦编著的巨著《吕氏春秋·季秋纪》记载：农历九月，大雁从北飞到南方，菊开出黄灿灿的花朵，豺在这时开始捕捉小的飞禽走兽。天子召见群臣，命令主管官员，严明号令，各级官员无论级别高低，都必须致力于收敛纳藏大事，以顺应天地秋季肃杀闭藏万物的旨意，不可有散逸外泄之事。还命令掌管帝王家财务及宫内事务的官员，在农事结束之后，必须统计五谷收成情况并记入账簿，将天子进行过籍田仪式的收入藏入神仓之中。还要举行祭祀上天的仪式，奉献牲畜请上天享用。可见当时已有在秋季九月农作物丰收之时祭飨天帝、祭祖，以谢天帝、祖先恩德的活动。

（二）重阳节的形成时期

重阳节的节日化、世俗化是在西汉初期完成的。在这个过程中，重阳节融合了多种民俗因素及神秘观念，逐渐确定了避邪求寿和秋季狂欢的内涵。一般认为西汉之前重阳节的一些习俗可能只在宫中流传。传说汉朝开国皇帝刘邦和宠妾戚夫人在长安宫边饮菊花酒边下棋。刘邦去世后，戚夫人被吕后害死，戚夫人的贴身侍女贾佩兰被驱逐出宫后将重阳节习俗传播到民间，重阳节遂逐渐成为一个全国性的节日。

在汉代，已经出现了重阳节佩戴茱萸、饮菊花酒、登高等风俗内容。古人将茱萸作为驱邪的神物，在重阳节人人都要佩戴，后世称之为"茱萸会"，故又称重阳节为"茱萸节"。菊花凌霜不谢，傲寒而开，气味芬芳，被认为是延年益寿的佳品，因此菊花酿成的酒无论是宗室贵族还是达官商贾无不喜欢，也是重阳节必不可少的饮品。随着节日规模的扩大，活动内容也日渐丰富多彩，重阳节在民众生活中的地位也越来越重要，随之而来的后世重阳节的相应习俗在这一时期已经相当完备，重阳习俗完全形成。

魏晋六朝是一个社会大动荡、大分裂的时代。这段时期，分分合合、战乱频繁，民众的生命财产得不到切实的保障，人们对生命苦短的恐惧使得以祛除灾患、祈福求寿为内涵的重阳节日益受到重视。此时的人们更加意识到生命的珍贵，更加看重现实生活的享乐和亲情的抒发。此时，还出现了许多关于重阳节的诗词。

晋朝陶渊明也与重阳节有着千丝万缕的关系。其中最为有名的是白衣送酒的故事。有一年重阳节，陶渊明在东篱下赏菊，抚琴吟唱，忽而酒兴大发。由于没有备酒过节，他只好漫步菊丛，采摘了一大束菊花，坐在屋旁惆怅。就在这时，他看见一个白衣使者向他走来，一问才知此人是江州刺史王弘派来送酒的。王弘喜欢结交天下名士，曾多次给陶渊明送酒。陶渊明大喜，立即开坛畅饮，酒酣而诗兴起，吟出了《九日闲居》这一首名诗。

○ 陶渊明纪念馆

旅游小贴士

陶渊明纪念馆

陶渊明纪念馆位于江西省九江市九江县沙河街东北隅，是历史人物纪念馆，为纪念东晋诗人陶渊明而建立。该馆占地 1600 平方米。馆内辟有《陶渊明生平事略陈列》，收藏和展出有关陶渊明行踪的图表、照片、家谱和历代陶学专著、名人书画 300 多件。景点有：归来亭、陶靖节祠、陶渊明墓。

（三）重阳节的鼎盛时期

唐宋时期，是重阳节发展的鼎盛时期。重阳节自出现以来，一直受到上层统治者的重视和下层民众的喜爱，但是，直到唐代中叶，才被最高统治者正式定名为"重阳节"，成为法定的"三令节"之一。唐朝规定三令节为法定休息日，还为官员集体游乐提供经费。唐代重阳节的繁荣主要体现在诗歌创作上，那时，重阳诗已经成熟，并且非常盛行。

宋代比较注重赏菊，宫内每到九月八日就开始欢度重九了，除在庆瑞殿中摆列色彩缤纷的菊花珍品外，还燃起菊花灯，摆下赏灯宴，故重阳节在宋代堪称"菊花节"。在这一时期，形成的重阳民俗主要有：郊游宴饮、曲江饮宴、重阳竞射等民俗活动。

1. 郊游宴饮

唐代民间以重九郊游野宴为主。唐代著名医药学家孙思邈在《千金方·月令》中写道，在重阳节这天，一定要带上美酒佳肴登高远眺。酒中还要配上茱萸和菊花。北宋时，朝廷九月初九这天要举行盛大的祭祀仪式，所以大举重阳宴，宫厨忙着做"重阳糕"。

2. 曲江饮宴

唐代京城长安过重阳节的时候，上自皇帝百官，下至平民百姓，都喜欢去曲江池饮宴。所谓"曲江"，即曲江园林，位于今陕西西安东南，汉武帝造宜春苑于此，隋朝改名芙蓉园。唐复名曲江，号称都中第一胜景。当时水域面积颇大，碧波粼粼，彩舟竞渡。四周有数不清的可供观景的亭台楼阁，遍种名树、花卉。贵族和文人雅士

○曲江池

趋之若鹜，帝王也经常游赏饮宴于此。每逢三月三日、中元节、重阳节，皇室贵族、达官显贵都来此游赏，樽壶酒浆、笙歌画船、宴乐于曲江水上。

3. 重阳竞射

在古代，人们喜欢在重阳节时开展骑射游乐。南北朝时，皇廷曾规定每年的重阳时，武官们必须练习骑马射箭，并把骑马射箭作为一种武举应试项目，只有步射与骑射都及格了，才能参加其他项目的考试。唐代时朝廷允许五品以上的官员，齐集于玄武门练习骑射。至清代时，骑射更成为满族官吏、八旗兵士及王府子弟必须熟习的一项武功，清末时北京就曾建有很多赛马场，射猎、射箭、骑射、赛马曾成为老北京城重阳等民俗节

○国画"重阳节骑射"

日里必有的比武游乐项目。

（四）现代发展为"老人节""敬老节"

20世纪80年代起，中国一些地方把农历九月初九日定为老人节，倡导全社会形成尊老、敬老、爱老、助老的风气。1989年，中国政府将农历九月初九定为"老人节""敬老节"。2006年5月20日，重阳节经国务院批准列入第一批国家级非物质文化遗产。2012年12月28日，全国人大常委会表决通过新修改的《老年人权益保障法》。法律明确，每年农历九月初九为"老年节"，九月为"敬老月"。

中国已经进入人口老龄化社会，组织开展"敬老月"活动有利于全社会积极应对人口老龄化。敬老活动主要包括走访慰问、老年维权、老年文化体育活动、老龄宣传活动等。到九月初九这一天，全国各机关、团体，都会组织退休的员工秋游赏景，登山健体。不少晚辈也会搀扶着年老的长辈到郊外活动，或者为老人准备一些可口的饮食。

○ 成都理工大学青年志愿者在2013年重阳节赴社区养老院开展志愿服务活动（程士涛 摄）

I

The Origin and Inheritance of the Double Ninth Festival

The Double Ninth Festival (Chongyang Festival), a traditional Chinese holiday, falls on Sept. 9 in the Chinese lunar calendar. It is also called "Height Ascending Festival", "Zhuyu Festival", "Senior Citizens' Day" or "Daughters' Day". On this day, people will climb mountains, appreciate chrysanthemum, wear *zhuyu*, have Double Ninth cake, and fly kites. What does "Double Ninth" mean? How did the festival get its names? How has it evolved in the long history of China? In the following you'll get the answers.

1. The Origin of the Double Ninth Festival

According to the ancient Chinese people's philosophy, all of the things under the heaven are categorized into *yin* and *yang*, with the former for darkness and the latter for brightness. This applies to numbers, too, which are categorized into *yin* and *yang* correspondingly. Actually *yin* figures are even while *yang* odd. Hence, nine is a *yang* figure. In the Chinese calendar, the ninth day of the ninth month means "Double Ninth" or "Double *Yang*", hence the name. It's found that the Double Ninth Festival originated from the distant ancient time, was officially celebrated in the Spring and Autumn Period (722 B.C. —481 B.C.), prevailed in the West Han Dynasty, and reached its zenith in the Tang Dynasty. The Double Ninth Festival can also be called "Autumn Hiking Day", a counterpart of "Spring Hiking Day" on Mar. 3 in the Chinese lunar calendar, when people go for hiking, ascending a height, and enjoying autumn and spring sceneries. That's why it has got the following names: Height Ascending Festival, Chrysanthemum Festival, Zhuyu Festival, Senior Citizens' Day, etc.

Since the two nines in the ninth day of the ninth month has the same pronunciation with another Chinese expression *jiujiu* (means forever) and nine is the biggest single-digit figure, the Double Ninth Festival is equipped with the implication of longevity. So people will worship ancestors and promote the activities of revering the elderly people. The Double Ninth Festival, along with the Chinese Lunar New Year's Eve, the

Tomb Sweeping Day, and the Ghost Festival, are the four festivals when Chinese people worship their ancestors.

As for the origin and history of the Double Ninth Festival, there're a lot of different sayings about them since it originated from the remote times.

1.1 Celebrations of September in the remote ancient times

In the ancient agricultural times, people basically finished their harvesting and had adequate time for leisure in September of the Chinese lunar calendar . That's why the ancient Chinese people chose September for celebrating harvest and offering sacrifices.

According to the *Autumn Volume of Master Lv's Spring and Autumn Annals*, the ancient people began to hold activities for celebrating harvesting as well as offering sacrifices to heaven, earth, and ancestors, which were stipulated and written into ordinances by the rulers in the Spring and Autumn Period.

These celebrations contained obvious elements of entertainment and carnival such as drinking wine, going out for a picnic, singing and dancing, etc. This well explains how the Double Ninth customs after the Han Dynasty came into being. It's no wonder that people will call the September celebration of the pre-Qin Era as "The God of Wine Day". This is the most possible origin of the Double Ninth Festival.

1.2 The Worship of the God of Fire of the pre-Qin Era

One of the stereotypes of the Double Ninth Festival is the

observation of offering sacrifices to fire, which the primitive people worshipped most since they believed that it could bring about light and warmness.

The ancient Chinese people called one of the brightest constellations as Xinsu'er Star and regarded it as the incarnation of the God of Fire, and hence it got another name "the Great Mars". People, by observing its movement, identified the change of seasons.

Due to its function of distinguishing four seasons, the legend has that, more than four thousand years ago, Zhuanxu, a monarch of the ancient China, set an official to watch this constellation. When it comes to September, the star, the symbol of the seasonal change, would retreat, which meant the approaching of the winter. In this season, a lot of primitive ancestors would die of coldness and hunger for their invulnerability against weather and lack of food. However, they believed it was because of the retreatment of the God of Fire that induced demons and monsters, running wild. So, people held varieties of ceremonies to offer sacrifices to the God of Fire for security. Although we know very little about those rituals, we can still find out some ancient traces from the existing ceremonies of the Double Ninth Festival; for example, the practice of offering sacrifices to the God of Kitchen is kept in some regions south of the Yangtze River.

The worship of fire in the pre-Qin Era is an important origin for praying for longevity and scaring off the evil during the Double Ninth Festival. In the meanwhile, those activities of offering sacrifices have become important components of China's agricultural civilization.

> **Background information**
>
> ## Offering sacrifices to the God of Kitchen
>
> Offering sacrifices to the God of Kitchen is a prevailing and influential traditional Chinese custom. Many families set a niche for the God of Kitchen, which is called Siming Buddha (Buddha of fate) or Zhaojun Buddha (Buddha of the God of Kitchen). The legend has that this God, appointed by the Jade Emperor, a superior ruler of the people on the earth, was responsible for managing kitchen fire. He was worshipped as the God of protecting a whole family. The niche for the God of Kitchen is generally set in the middle of the northern or eastern wall of the kitchen. If without the sculpture of the God of Kitchen, people will stick his picture on the wall. Sometimes there's only the God of Kitchen; sometimes there're two Gods of the Kitchen, with another one being Grandma God of the Kitchen. The God of Kitchen is the most typical deity, deeply–rooted in masses, to whom people pray for blessings and driving away the evils.
>
> People offer sacrifices to the God of Kitchen usually on the 23rd or 24th of December of the lunar calendar while some parts south of the Yangtze River on the Double Ninth Festival.

1.3 Tales and legends

The origins of the Double Ninth Festival are closely related to tales and legends just as the other traditional Chinese holidays.

1) Huan Jing fighting against the Monster of Plague

Monstrous and Mysterious Stories, Continued written by Wu Jun of the Southern Dynasties (420 A.D.-589 A.D.) recorded the following story. In the East Han Dynasty, there was a man, Huan Jing, who lived in Runan County of Henan Province with his family by living on farming peacefully. But a storm might arise from a clear sky. A plague hit the reaches of the Ru River and took away a lot of people's lives. Huan Jing recalled that when he was a child, the elders told him that the Monster of Plague living in the Ru River spread plague annually. To kill the monster for his countrymen, Huan Jing went out to seek immortals and succeeded in finding an immortal named Fei Zhangfang. He decided to visit him.

Although he crossed numerous rivers and climbed over numerous mountains, Huan Jing could find no trace of the immortal. One day, suddenly he saw a snow-white pigeon keep nodding at him in front of him. He went close to it and only saw it fly several meters away, landed on the earth, and began nodding at him again. In this way, he followed the pigeon and arrived at the immortal's dwelling. He knelt before the gate devoutly for two days and nights. On the third day, the gate was opened and a gray-haired old man said to him smilingly: "I know you're earnest in saving your countrymen. Please follow me."

Fei gave Huan Jing the Dark Dragon Sword of Subduing Demons and Monsters and taught him practice mysteries of defeating the monster. One day, when Huan Jing was playing swords, Fei came to tell him: "On this Sept. 9th, the Monster of Plague in the Ru River will go out and spread plague again. You must hurry back home and fight against it. Here's a packet of zhuyu leaves and a bottle of chrysanthemum wine. Give them to your countrymen and ask them to climb to the top of the mountain for hiding from the monster." Then, he summoned a crane to fly Huan Jing home.

After he went back home, Huan Jing conveyed what Fei said to his countrymen. Upon Sept. 9th, he led them for climbing onto the top of a nearby mountain, the Gangshan Mountain with a length of 25 km, a width of 7 km, and a height of 97.2 km during the Spring and Autumn Period. It's the highest one in Shangcai County of Henan Province and named the Lugang Mountain.

Huan Jing distributed the zhuyu leaves to everyone, which scared off the monster. He shared the chrysanthemum wine with the others, too, which could prevent them from catching plague. After everything was settled, he came back home with the Dark Dragon Sword of Subduing Demons and Monsters, waiting for the monster.

Soon after, with the wind howling and the Ru River roaring, the Monster of Plague walked out of the river and went onto the bank. As soon as he saw the crowd on the top of the mountain, he dashed to its foot but was scared off by the aroma of wine and the pungent smell of the zhuyu leaves. As he turned his head over, Huan Jing drew out of the sword and fought against him for a few rounds. The Monster of Plague was soon defeated and ran away. Huan Jing threw out the glittering sword and nailed the monster dead on the earth within a blink of eye.

Thereafter, the people who lived in the reaches of the Ru River were exempt from being struck by the plague. The customs of height ascending for hiding from disasters, wearing zhuyu, drinking chrysanthemum wine on Sept. 9th have been carried on unto today.

Runan County in the legend is Shangcai County of today's Henan Province. Therefore, this county is regarded as the origin of China's Double Ninth Festival. In 2003, the Chinese Post Administration held the debut of the special Double Ninth Festival stamps. In Dec. of 2005, Shangcai County was named "The Home of the Double Ninth Culture", the only one in China. In March of 2006 of the Gregorian calendar, the Double Ninth customs were included on the list of the first batch of intangible cultural heritages by the Henan provincial government. In June of 2011, it was included on the list of the third batch of national intangible cultural heritages by the State Council. Shangcai county boasts its long history, plenty of scenic spots and cultural interests, and numerous talents. It's a place where the Chinese ancient civilization begins and the Chinese traditional cultures converge. It's said in the ancient times, Fuxi, the ancestor of the Chinese people, drew the Eight Diagrams which represented the Chinese ancient philosophy by observing the things under heaven. After that, he taught people knitting net for fishing, taming household animals, learning from the principles of heaven and earth. His descendants built the Fuxi Temple to express their gratitude to him and commemorate him at Caihe, the ancient Cai Kingdom, located in today's Shangcai County with a history of more than 3 thousand years.

2) The Lishan Mountain Tale

The tale had it that long long ago there was a farmer who lived with his family at the foot of the Lishan Mountain. They were hard-working, but they could only make ends meet.

One day, the farmer came back home from his land and encountered a fortune-teller on the way who was seeking for accommodation since it was soon dark. The farmer's house was a small thatched hut. He had to move his wife and children to the kitchen and let them sleep on a spread of straw. He, himself, slept on the bed with the fortune-teller.

When it was dawn the next day, before the fortune-teller left, the farmer woke up his wife for making a rich breakfast for the former and gave him a bag of steamed buns. The fortune-teller went out of the hut, had a glimpse of the surrounding environment, and told the farmer, "Take your family to the height on the Double Ninth day." The farmer was wondering why he said so since he had no ambition of being promoted to the higher social position. But he got to the point soon: maybe there would be some troubles for his dwelling since the fortune-teller was good at *fengshui* and astronomy. He was determined to take his family to the height on that day, at least for the sake of scenery.

On the Double Ninth day, the farmer led his family in climbing the Lishan Mountain by taking with them the flower cakes (rice cake with flower patterns) and wine. After they arrived at the top of the mountain, a spring gushed from the middle of the mountain and washed away their thatched hut. Very soon, the whole valley was immersed in water. The farmer finally knew why the fortune-teller told them to climb onto the top of the mountain.

After the story was spread, people would go for height ascending on the Double Ninth Festival and thus the custom was carried on.

Lishan Mountain Scenery

Tourist tips

The Lishan Mountain

The Lishan Mountain, a well-known tourist scenic spot in China, is located in the south of the Lintong County of Xi'an City in Shanxi Province, more than 30 kms away from the downtown of Xi'an City. It's a branch of the Qinlin Mountains, extending from west to east for 25 kms, north to south for 13.7 kms with an altitude of 1.302 kms. The mountain, covered with luxuriant pines and shades of green, looks like a steed, and hence the name Lishan (Li for steed; shan for mountain). It's an important component of the Huaqing Palace scenic spot and a famous Taoist mountain which boasts numerous historical and cultural interests and beautiful natural sceneries. Since the Zhou, Qin, Han, and Tang Dynasties, it had been the royal garden with plenty of palaces and halls.

Address: 3 East Ring Road, Lintong District, Xi'an City

2. The Inheritance of the Double Ninth Festival

The Double Ninth Festival came into being as early as in the Spring and Autumn Period and was officially set as a civil festival in the Tang Dynasty. Since then, it has been observed through the later dynasties until today. On the Double Ninth day the whole family will go for "the Autumn Hiking" just as they do for "the Spring Hiking" on Mar. 3rd in the Chinese lunar calendar. The celebrations of the Double Ninth Festival include: autumn hiking, climbing mountains, enjoying chrysanthemums, wearing zhuyu, having the Double Ninth cake, drinking the chrysanthemum wine, etc.

2.1 The beginning period of the Double Ninth Festival

The Double Ninth Festival can date back to the days in the pre-Qin Era. According to the *Autumn Volumn of Master Lv's Spring and Autumn Annals*, in September of the lunar calendar, wild geese migrated from north to south, sparrows dived in the sea and became into clams, chrysanthemums bloomed in golden color, and leopards began to prey on birds and animals. At this moment, the monarch summoned the officials and commanded them to abstain from sex for saving energy no matter how privileged they were by conforming to the law of heaven and earth. All of the things under heaven stopped intercourse and hid during the autumn season. He also ordered the officials who managed the financial affairs of the royal families and the court affairs to have a statistics of the harvest and keep accounts, and to store the harvest of the monarch's land into the exclusive warehouse for sacrifice grains. The ceremonies of offering sacrifices to heaven were held and the livestock was offered to heaven. This is origin of offering sacrifices to heaven and ancestors on the Double Ninth day.

2.2 The forming period of the Double Ninth Festival

The Double Ninth Festival was officially set in the West Han Dynasty. In this process, it absorbed varieties of folk customs and mysteries and gradually developed the connotations of scaring off the evils, praying for longevity and spending the autumn carnival. It's generally believed that some traditions only prevailed in the court before the Western Han

Dynasty. It was said that the first emperor of the Han Dynasty, Liu Bang, with his beloved concubine, Madame Qi, played chess while drinking chrysanthemum wine beside the Chang'an (eternal peace) Palace and bet the winner would live a long life. After Liu Bang died, Madame Qi was prosecuted dead by his Empress, Madame Lv, and the former's maid, Jia Peilan, driven away from the court, took the Double Ninth Festival traditions to the folks. Then the Double Ninth Festival had gradually become a national holiday.

In the Han Dynasty, the traditions of wearing zhuyu, drinking chrysanthemum wine, climbing mountains had taken shape. The ancient people deemed zhuyu as the sacred thing of driving away the evil spirits and would wear it on the Double Ninth Festival, which was called "zhuyu Party" by the descendants, hence it got another name: zhuyu Festival. The chrysanthemum was thought to be the elixir for health and longevity since it braved autumn frost, nourished, and smelled fragrantly. So the chrysanthemum wine, a must for the Double Ninth Festival, was greatly applauded by the royal family members, high-rank officials, and merchants. With the escalation of the festival's connotations, more traditions were developed and its position was greatly lifted accordingly. We can simply say that it was during this period that the Double Ninth Festival customs had completely formed.

The Six Dynasties Period (222 A.D.—589 A.D.) witnessed great turbulence and division. During this period, with the wars raging on and people's lives and properties being under frequent threats, their fear of premature death made prominent the Double Ninth Festival featuring praying for blessings and longevity while driving away the evil spirits and avoiding disaster. The people who lived in the tumultuous times were more keenly aware of the value of life and tended to indulge in worldly pleasure and value more kinship. In the meanwhile, a lot of poems on the Double Ninth Festival were written.

Tao Yuanming of the Jin Dynasty (265 A.D.—420 A.D.) was closely related to this festival. The most famous story was *Baiyi Songjiu*, which means a man dressed in white sent wine to Tao. On one Double Ninth Festival, when Tao was enjoying chrysanthemums in his garden, singing by playing *qin* (a musical instrument), suddenly a strong desire for wine occurred to him. But he did not prepare any, he had to wander among the chrysanthemums and pick some of them, sighing melancholy in his garden. It was at this moment that an envoy dressed in white walked to him. He was dispatched by Wang Hong, the Jiangzhou governor, for presenting wine to Tao. Wang was fond of getting in with men of letters and had ever sent wine to Tao for many times. Tao was intoxicated with the wine and wrote the famous poem, *A Leisured Life on the Double Ninth*. Here're several lines taken from this poem:

"The wine relieves me of many a care;

Chrysanthemums give me years to spare.

How can I, a wretched scholar, stand alone

And let the time flow forward on its own!"

Tao Yuanming's Memorial

Tao Yuanming's Memorial is located in the north-east of Shahe Street of Jiujiang County, Jiangxi Province, occupying 1600 square meters. There're exhibitions of Tao's life stories, including more than 300 relics such as figures, tablets, pictures, Tao's family tree, monographs on Tao studies, celebrities' calligraphy and paintings, etc.

Scenic spots: Returning Home Pavilion; Tao Yuanming Temple; Tao Yuanming's Cemetery

2.3 The prime period of the Double Ninth Festival

In the Tang and Song dynasties, the Double Ninth Festival reached its zenith. Since the appearance of this festival, it had been favored by the upper-class rulers and the lower-class people; however, it was officially recognized as the Double Ninth Festival until the mid-Tang Dynasty and became one of the legitimate San Ling Jie (Three legitimate festivals). The Tang Dynasty stipulated the San Ling Jie as legitimate holidays and even offered fee for officials' entertainment. The blooming of the Double Ninth Festival in the Tang Dynasty was mainly represented in poems which reached its zenith, too.

The Song Dynasty gave priority to chrysanthemum appreciation. The court began to celebrate the Double Ninth Festival on Sept. 8th. The precious chrysanthemum flowers were exhibited at the Qingrui Palace, the chrysanthemum lanterns were lit, and the banquet for watching lanterns were arranged. Thus, the Double Ninth Festival was called "the Chrysanthemum Festival". During this period, the following traditions came into being: going out for picnic, banquet at the Qujiang Pond, and Double Ninth shooting and racing, etc.

1) Going out for picnic

In the Tang Dynasty the common people generally went for picnic on Sept. 9th. The famous doctor of the Tang Dynasty Sun Simiao wrote in his medical masterpiece, *The Monthly Remedies of A Thousand Gold Prescriptions*: on Sept. 9th, people must bring fine wine with chrysanthemum and zhuyu and food with them and climb mountains. In the Northern Song Dynasty, the court would hold grand ceremonies to offer sacrifices on this day and the Double Ninth Banquet was hosted, too. The royal chefs were busy with making Double Ninth Cake.

2) Banquet at the Qujiang Garden

On the Double Ninth day, the emperors, officials, and the common people would go to the Qujiang Pond for feasting. The Qujiang Garden, located in south-east of Xi'an City of Shanxi Province, where the Emperor Wudi of the Han Dynasty built the Yichun Garden, was named Furong Garden (Hibiscus Garden) and restored to Qujiang Garden again in the Tang Dynasty. It was crowned as the first scenic resort of the capital. During the Tang Dynasty, the pond with a vast area of water shimmered in the sunlight and the painted boats raced on it. Pavilions, terraces, and towers surrounded the pond and precious trees and flowers were thriving. The noblemen and men of letters were fascinated with the garden and the emperors feasted here, too. On the Spring Hiking Festival, the Ghost Festival, and the Double Ninth Festival, the royal family members, noblemen, officials, and men of letters would tour the Qujiang Garden, feasting, and singing or playing musical instruments on the beautifully painted boats.

Qujiang Pond

3) Double Ninth shooting on horse

In the ancient times, people used to ride horses and shoot for amusement. In the Southern and Northern Dynasties, the royal court ordered that the military officials should practice horse-riding and shooting, which were included in examination on recruiting the military officials. The examinees could be qualified for the other subjects only if they passed shooting on land and shooting on horse. In the Tang Dynasty, the officials of above level-5 rank were allowed to practice shooting on horse. In the Qing Dynasty, shooting on horse had become a must for the Manchu officials, the Eight Banner soldiers, and the royal family members. During that time, there were a lot of horse-racing courses. Hunting, shooting, shooting on horse, and horse-racing were primary entertainment games in the old Beijing on the Double Ninth Festival.

4) Evolution into Senior Citizens' Day

Since 1980s, some parts of China set Sept. 9th as the Senior Citizens' Day to advocate respecting, loving, and assisting the elder people. In 1989, the Chinese government set this day as the Senior Citizens' Day or Revering the Elders Day. In May 20 of 2006, the Double Ninth Festival was included on the list of the first batch of national intangible cultural heritages. In Dec. 12 of 2012, the Standing Committee of the National People's Congress of China voted for the newly-amended Law on the *Protection of the Rights and Interests of the Elderly* which stipulated that Sept 9th is the Senior Citizens' Day and every September is the Month for the Elderly.

Since China has entered the threshold of the aged society, organizing various activities in the Month for the Elderly, including visiting the elderly, maintaining the rights and interests of the elderly, gathering the elderly for cultural and sports activities, and promotional activities etc., helps coping with the aging problems. On the Double Ninth day, the administrative organs and social groups at all levels will organize the retired staff members for autumn hiking and climbing mountains. The children will accompany the elderly to go for autumn hiking or prepare some tasty food for them.

The Elderly Theatrical Performance Organized by Cangyi Road Community, Qingdao City, Shandong Province on 2010 Double Ninth Festival (from the Qingdao Network)

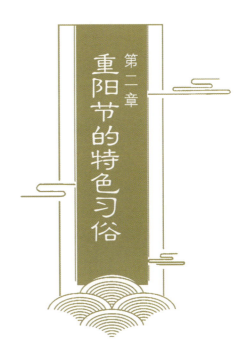

第二章

重阳节的特色习俗

　　金秋送爽，丹桂飘香，农历九月初九的重阳佳节，活动丰富、热闹非凡。重阳节在长期的文化积淀和凝聚过程中，经历了几千年的文化筛选逐渐成为中华民族的传统节日，形成了今天吃重阳糕、佩戴茱萸、赏菊饮酒、登高望远、放纸鸢、祭奠先祖的习俗。

一、
重阳节食俗

（一）食重阳糕

　　重阳食糕是重阳节的代表性习俗，它同样是"登高"谐音的民俗表达。

　　糕是一种食品，主要由稻米粉蒸成，是人们待客、祭祀的佳品。重阳糕又称花糕、菊糕、五色糕，做法各地不同。在古代，到了重阳

○山东阳谷农民制作的九层重阳糕（张振祥　摄）

节前后，秋收完毕，大家为了欢庆丰收，家家户户用面粉做些米糕馈赠亲朋好友。人们在用面粉做出的蒸糕上插上彩色的小旗子，点缀上石榴子、栗子、松子仁等果实。用发面做的重阳糕，如今称为"蒸糕"，松甜软糯，十分可口。

九月食糕的习俗起源很早，在汉朝时称为"饵"。饵的原料是米粉，米粉有稻米粉与黍米粉两种，黍米有黏性，两者放在一起蒸，蒸出的食物就称为"饵"。黍是中国古代一种非常重要的粮食作物，是古人待客与祭祀的佳品。九月，黍谷成熟，人们用黍米作为应时的尝新食品。古人对祖先非常尊敬，因此，首先以用生活中最重要的食品黍祭祀先人。我们现在食用的重阳糕的前身就是古人九月的尝新食品。这也就是后世民间在重阳节以重阳糕拜神祭祖的秋祭习俗的渊源。

约从宋代开始，重阳节吃"重阳糕"的习俗已经正式被记载入册，如宋代文人吴自牧在他写的一本介绍南宋都城临安城市风貌的著作《梦粱录》里记载了重阳节的习俗："此日都人店肆以糖面蒸糕……插小彩旗，名曰'重阳糕'。"这种插小旗于花糕上的传统，至今流传。

现在的重阳糕，做法各地不尽相同，没有固定的品种，各地在

○ 重阳糕上插小旗

重阳节这天吃的松软的糕类都称为重阳糕。因为"糕"与"高"同音，吃糕有高升的寓意，因而备受人们的青睐。讲究的糕要做成九层，象征宝塔，象征"九重天"。而有的地方则是把重阳糕用红、黑、黄、白、青五种颜色来装饰，其寓意就是为了辟邪。古人对这五种颜色极其喜爱，认为是世间的五种原色，并迷信其功效，认为能够驱灾辟邪。重阳糕不仅自家食用，也被用来馈赠亲友。

重阳这天把出嫁的女儿接回家里吃糕，称为"归宁"。成书于明朝末期的《帝京景物略》中记载，每到重阳，出嫁女子的父母家一定要迎女儿回家吃花糕。如果哪家没有这么做，那女子的家人就会受到谴责，所以重阳节也被称为"女儿节"。

关于食花糕的起源有两种说法，一种是说宋高祖刘裕纂晋之前，有一年在一个叫作彭城的地方过重阳节。他一时兴起，便骑马登上了西楚霸王项羽在彭州所搭建的戏马台上。等他即位称帝后，便规定每年九月九日为骑马射箭、校阅军队的日子。据传说，后来流行的重阳糕，就是当年发给士兵的干粮。

旅游小贴士

徐州戏马台

戏马台位于江苏省徐州市中心区户部山最高处，原是徐州最负盛名的古迹之一。公元前 206 年，盖世英雄项羽灭秦后自立为西楚霸王，定都彭城（即今徐州），于城南的南山上，因山为台，以观戏马、演武和阅兵等，故名戏马台。

地址：江苏省徐州市云龙区项王路 1 号

另一种传说则流传于陕西附近。传说明朝的状元康海是陕西武功人。他参加八月中的乡试后，卧病长安。八月下旨放榜后，报喜的报子兼程将此喜讯送到武功，但此时康海还未抵家。家里没人打发赏钱，报子就不肯走，一定要等到康海回来。等康海病好回家时，已经是重阳节了。这时他才打发报子，给了他赏钱，并蒸了一锅糕给他回程作干粮。又多蒸了一些糕分给左邻右舍。因为这糕是用来庆祝康海中状元，所以后来有子弟上学的人家，也在重阳节蒸糕分发，讨一个"步步高升"的好兆头。

重阳糕不仅自家食用，还馈送亲友，称"送糕"。重阳节制作和食用重阳糕的习俗一直流传至今，他们通过这样的方式在庆祝节日的同时，祈求家人和朋友平安健康。在北京、陕西、山东该习俗最为突出。

旧时老北京花糕种类繁多，一类是饽饽铺里卖的烤制好的酥饼糕点，

○ 老北京花糕

如糟子糕、桃酥、碗糕、蛋糕、萨其马等；一类是四合院里主妇们、农村妇女用黄白米面蒸的金银蜂糕，糕上码有花生仁、杏仁、松子仁、核桃仁、瓜子仁等五仁；还有的是用油脂和面的蒸糕；将米粉染成五色的五色糕；还有的糕中夹铺着枣、糖、葡萄干、果脯，或在糕上撒些猪肉丝、鸡鸭肉丝，再贴上"吉祥"或"福寿禄禧"字样，并插上五彩花旗。人们买回花糕供于佛堂、祠堂或作为礼品馈赠亲友。

在陕西，重阳节当天除流行送"花糕"外，还会赠送"曲连"。这两种食物都是用上等麦面粉制成的。不同的是用锅蒸的叫"花糕"，用鏊烤烙的叫"曲连"。糕，一般是圆形或椭圆形，由底向上共三至五层乃至七层，逐渐升高。糕者谐音"高"，步步高升之意。每层周围都涂制花朵，糕顶更是百花盛开，争奇斗艳。这样的花馍就叫作"花糕"。"曲连"是烙制成的糕，花样多，如玉环、镰刀、斧头等，曲曲弯弯连接在一起，所以叫作"曲连"。"花糕"和"曲连"的送法：首先是一个大型的"花糕"或曲连，再配带几个小"花糕"或小"曲连"。送双不送单（大者主糕除外），一般有一个孩子的，送二至四个小"花糕"（曲连）。有两个孩子的，送六至八个小"花糕"（曲连）。小"花糕"名为"耍糕"，是送给小孩玩耍的食品。

在山东，花糕以面蒸做，双层中夹以枣、栗之类果品，单层枣、栗插于面上，有的还插上彩色小纸旗，谓"花糕旗"，有的上安两只面塑的羊，取重阳之意，谓"重阳花糕"。花糕既是节日食品，又是节日赠品，济南以北地区不仅送糕，还送秋冬应用的衣物。

○山东曲连

（二）吃米果，尝蟹黄

在福建莆仙，人们沿袭旧俗，要蒸九层的重阳米果，我国古代就有重阳"食饵"之俗，"饵"就是今天的糕点、米果一类的食物。

○春米浆

清初莆仙诗人宋祖谦《闽酒曲》曰："惊闻佳节近重阳，纤手携篮拾野香。玉杵捣成绿粉湿，明珠颗颗唤郎尝。"近代以来，人们又把米果改制为一种很有特色的九重米果。将优质晚米用清水淘洗，浸泡2小时，捞出沥干，掺水磨成稀浆，加入明矾（用水溶解）搅拌，加红板糖（掺水熬成糖浓液），而后置蒸笼于锅上，铺上洁净炊布，然后分九次，舀入米果浆，蒸若干时即熟出笼，米果面抹上花生油。此米果分九层重叠，可以揭开，切成菱形，四边层次分明，呈半透明状，食之甜软适口，又不粘牙，堪称重阳敬老的最佳礼物。节日期间，福州还有一种特制的糕点，称为九重粿，即粿有9层，中间夹7层糖色，寓意节节高升和登高消灾。

○刚刚出笼的九重粿

在扬州重阳节吃的重阳糕也

○重阳糕

是必备的时令食品。糕是米粉做成的，蒸熟即食，微甜、松软、爽口，老人和孩童很喜欢吃。糕形也很有趣，多是正方形，小小巧巧的，上染红点。卖糕人把若干块小糕叠成一摞，最上面插着一面纸质小旗。小旗有红有绿，呈三角形，还戳有许多小孔。戳了孔，较硬的小纸旗便柔软多了，迎风还能飘动。这就是所谓的"重阳旗"。旧时，扬州的重阳糕比现今的更精致。《真州竹枝词引》中就记述了一位名叫"萧美人"的店家，每到九月九日重阳时，就做萧美人糕，以此名重一时，这里的萧美人糕也就是如今的重阳糕。《真州竹枝词引》还记载了当时制作重阳糕的方式，在菊花糕上插上红绿纸旗，称为重阳旗，还会用糕面做出小亭子、小羊，形态各异，可谓是一件精美又好吃的艺术品。

在中国秦岭—淮河以南的地区，江河纵横，湖泊遍地，水域面积较为广阔。重阳佳节正值农历九月，秋菊飘香，螃蟹膏满美味，肉质细嫩，正是食蟹的大好季节。在江苏徐州重阳节期间正是食蟹的好时间。传说，西周时即有"蟹酱"之类的食物出现，到了唐宋，更盛行清水煮蟹。古人常说：不到庐山就辜负了自己的眼睛，不吃螃蟹就辜负了自己的肚子。

宋代诗人梅尧臣有诗赞蟹："樽前已夺蟹滋味，当日莼羹枉对人。"金秋时节，螃蟹上市，秋蟹味道鲜美，江南阳澄湖等地的蟹格外有名，菜馆也会在农历九月间，推出以蟹肉制作的美味佳肴。时至今日，阳澄湖的清蒸大闸蟹闻名中外，在港、澳、台各家大餐馆里，均被列为农历九月时令佳肴。因为徐州靠近微山湖，那里有丰富的蟹源，所以多数徐州人都爱吃螃蟹，微山湖产的淡水蟹是徐州群众过中秋、重阳两大节日餐桌上不可少的佳肴。尤其是过重阳，没有肥蟹是难下菊花酒的。不少家庭担心重阳临近时买不到个头大的螃蟹，多是提前买到家，一个个用线绳捆住蟹脚，或用小号蒲草编成蒲包紧紧把蟹包住，洒上清水，保持湿润，可保证短期内鲜活。爱吃蟹还要会处理蟹，如处理不当，蒸或煮熟的螃蟹往往会蟹肢全掉，只剩下光秃秃的蟹身。这样是端不上餐桌的。为防止这种情况的发生，就必须一个个捆住蟹肢，以防螃蟹垂死挣扎，互相把蟹肢蹬掉。至于吃蟹的调料，因蟹属凉性，要多放姜末儿、米醋、少放点儿糖可以增其鲜味。全家人或和知己好友一起剥着鲜美的蟹肉，慢慢饮用着菊花浸泡过的美酒，拉着家常，叙谈亲朋间的亲情和友情，洋溢着浓浓的重阳节气氛。

　　绍兴是水乡，又临海，重阳节前后正是螃蟹大量上市之时，此

○重阳吃蟹

时的螃蟹肉嫩味美，价廉物美，因此，旧时绍兴还有重阳节吃螃蟹的习俗，民间也有"清明节吃螺丝，端午节吃虾，九月重阳节的时候吃横爬"的说法。"横爬"就是螃蟹，这是绍兴人对它形象而又幽默的称呼。

二、
重阳节佩俗

在众多重阳节习俗中，与登高关系最紧密的，要属佩戴茱萸了。茱萸是一种落叶小乔木，开小黄花，秋收后果实成熟，果实红色椭圆形，是一种常绿带香的植物，根、茎、叶和果实都能入药，具有杀虫消毒、逐寒祛风的功用，是一味有名的中药材。古时候人们还用茱萸根来治霍乱。明代李时珍所著的《本草纲目》说它气味辛辣芳香，性温热，可以治寒驱毒。

茱萸一开始叫作"吴萸"因为它原产自前秦的吴国。之后被改为"茱萸"，这里面还有一个有趣的小故事。

相传，在春秋战国时期，弱小的吴国每年都得按时向强邻楚国进贡。有一年，吴国的使者将本国的特产"吴萸"药材献给楚王。贪婪无知的楚王爱的是珍珠玛瑙金银财宝，根本看不起这土生土长的中药材，反认为是吴国在戏弄他，于是大发雷霆，不容吴国使者有半句解释，就令人将其赶出宫去。

楚王身边有位姓朱的大夫，与吴国使者交往甚密，忙将其接回家中，加以劝慰。吴国使者说，吴茱乃我国上等药材，有温中止痛、降逆止吐之功，善治胃寒腹痛、吐泻不止等症，因素闻楚王有胃寒腹痛的痼疾，故而献之，想不到楚王竟然不分青红皂白……听罢，朱大夫派人送吴国使者回国，并将他带来的吴茱精心保管起来。

次年，楚王受寒旧病复发，腹痛如刀绞，群医束手无策。朱大夫见时机已到，急忙将吴茱煎熬，献给楚王服下，片刻止痛，楚王大喜，重赏朱大夫，并询问这是什么药？朱大夫便将去年吴国使者献药之事叙述。楚王听后，非常懊悔，一面派人携带礼品向吴王道歉，一面命人广植吴茱。

几年后，楚国瘟疫流行，腹痛的病人遍布各地，全靠吴茱挽救成千上万百姓的性命。楚国百姓为感谢朱大夫的救命之恩，便在吴茱的前面加上一个"朱"字，改称"吴朱茱"。后世的医学家又在朱字上加个草字头，正式取名为"吴茱萸"，并一直沿用至今。因为茱萸特有的药用功效，古人认为佩带茱萸便可以辟邪去灾。

佩戴茱萸的方法有许多种。有人把它直接插在头上，有人先用

〇果实成熟的山茱萸

彩色的布做成红色的香囊，在香囊里面装上茱萸，再把装有茱萸的袋子缠在手臂上。晋朝周处《风土记》里说："九月九日，律中无射而数九，俗尚此日，折茱萸房以插头，言辟除恶气而御初寒。"这里详细地说明了古时佩戴茱萸的方法是"插"，而且"折茱萸房以插头"连插的部位也交代得很清楚。可见"插茱萸"的做法由来已久了。

而南朝吴均所著的《续齐谐记》记载了重阳节的传说，其中也说到"佩带茱萸"的事情：汝南（今河南省上蔡县）人桓景和费长房学道。一天，费长房对桓景说，九月九日那天，你家将有大灾，破解办法就是叫家人做一个红色的袋子，里面装上茱萸，缠在手臂上，然后登上高山，喝一些菊花酒，傍晚以后再回家。到了九月九日这一天，桓景照着师傅说的去做了。傍晚回家一看，果然家里的鸡犬牛羊都死了，全家人因为外出而避免了灾祸。于是茱萸"辟邪"的习俗也流传了下来，茱萸因此又被叫作"辟邪翁"。故事中详细地描述了佩戴茱萸的方法是"令家人各做绛（红色）囊，盛茱萸以系臂"。

茱萸绛囊作为一种民俗手工艺品，已经成为重阳节的一种标志物和符号。茱萸绛囊的起源地河南省上蔡县也将这一极具特色的手工艺品传承发扬，2006年上蔡县张社老人缝制的茱萸绛囊参加了在深圳举办的全国工艺品展销会。为将这一门手工技艺发扬光大，2006年，河南省人民政府将重阳茱萸绛囊的制作技艺列为第一批省级非物质文化遗产。

背景知识

图中的老人叫做张社，今年85岁的她是河南省"非遗"茱萸绛

囊代表性传承人，
她可缝制出 40 多个
品种的茱萸绛囊，
造型逼真、惟妙惟
肖。同时她还热心
传艺，已带出 40 多
名民间艺人。

○上蔡县张社老人制作的茱萸绛囊（来源：新华网）

　　无论以什么样的方法佩戴茱萸，这个习俗都深刻反映古代广大
穷苦百姓饱受病疫折磨，渴望摆脱疾病困扰的心情。于是，每逢佳节，
男女老少们便佩戴茱萸于头或臂，驱邪消灾，有些地方还将彩绸剪
成茱萸、菊花来相赠佩带。插茱萸，代表着人们对亲人健康平安的
美好期望，通常是家人或亲戚朋友之间相互赠送佩戴，以表达祝福。

三、
重阳节民俗

　　重阳节是杂糅多种民俗为一体而形成的中国传统节日。农历九
月初九前后，金风送爽，丹桂飘香，人们庆祝重阳节的方式很多，包
括出游赏景、登高远眺、赏菊品酒、遍插茱萸、吃重阳糕、扫墓祭祖等。

（一）登高

登高，是重阳节这一天举行的比较大型的活动，在古代，因为重阳有登高的习俗，所以重阳节又称"登高节"。金秋九月，天高气爽，遍地黄花，全家人团聚在一起，登上高高的山顶，欣赏深秋的美景。相传登高的风俗开始于东汉，在唐朝风行一时。许多著名的诗人为此留下了不少诗篇。杜甫的《登高》、崔国辅的《九月九日》都是描写重阳登高的名篇。因为能够登高望远，远在异乡的游子也能趁此机会远远眺望远方的家乡，由此重阳节也成了人们望乡思亲的时机。

重阳节登高的风俗历史悠久，其由来大致有三种说法：其一是登高避灾，其二是古人对山岳的崇拜，其三是由于重阳为秋季，节后树木开始凋零，所以登高野游是为"辞青"，与农历三月春游"踏青"相对应。

其实说到登高，最初是人类早期最直接的生存需求。古代先民以狩猎采集为生，群居洞穴山林。生存所需要的衣、食、住都来源于山林。高温炎热天气，大地像火烤一般炙热，人们躲进山间树林，可以躲避高温的袭击；洪水泛滥，人们登上高山避灾；高山云雾弥漫，而云气能致雨，观察到这一现象的原始先民以为山间有

○重阳登高

神明居住，有降雨的能力；高高的山峰高耸入云，人们以为是天上神仙住所的梯子，坚信只要攀到高山顶上，就能上天为神。原始先民对千变万化的自然现象，滋生了"万物有灵"的自然崇拜，对山的崇拜，对神的敬畏激发了人们登高、入仙境的强烈愿望。有学者认为，汉字崇拜的"崇"字，上为"山"下为"宗"（尊奉），说明"崇拜"一词原来很可能就是专对山岳而言的。

秦统一中国后，一直到汉朝，各朝的皇帝对山川祭祀都非常重视，帝王每年都要巡狩、祭祀名山大川。据史料记载，秦末时期，割据岭南建都番禺（今广州）的南越王赵佗，就曾登临越秀山，与君臣同乐。西汉闽越王无诸，也在九月九日率领将臣身配茱萸，登上福州的于山（古于越族所居处），饮菊花酒，一同游乐。所以于山又叫"九日山"。这些登高活动，比之前文讲到的桓景降魔，登高避祸的传说要早二百多年。

一年之中，秋季登高最好。此时秋高气爽，金菊飘香，亲朋好友相约结伴，身佩茱萸，携带佳酿，出外郊游，登高赏景。

老北京重阳盛行登高。古时皇帝在农历九月初九这一天，要亲

○重阳登高

自到万岁山（即景山）去登高拜佛祈求福寿平安，并观览京城风光，皇后妃子们则在故宫的御花园登临堆秀山登高眺望。清末的慈禧太后，每年重阳到北海东边的桃花山登高、野餐、烤肉，并支起蓝色的布架子防止人偷看。在民间，达官贵人、文人墨客或登临自家花园的假山亭台，或在旧京城内外爬山登高一览山景和京城的风景。那时老百姓登高主要是赴香山、五塔寺、景山公园等处所，一般全家或三、五好友一起。现在的北京人会在这一天，相约到香山、红螺山、百花山等植被茂盛、自然风光优美的地方登高赏秋。

旅游小贴士

北京香山

香山位于北京海淀区西郊，距市区 25 千米，顶峰香炉峰海拔 575 米，是北京著名的森林公园。2012 年被授予"世界名山"的称号，

○北京香山景色

是中国继泰山、黄山、庐山、峨眉山之后的第 5 座入选世界名山的中国名山。香山最著名的莫过于红叶胜景，深秋时节，漫山红叶，灿烂夺目，被评为"北京新十六景"之一。

最佳旅游季节：9 月~11 月最佳，霜降后香山红叶漫山遍野，此时的香山分外妖娆。

开放时间：06:00—18:30

地址：北京市海淀区西北郊小西山山脉东麓

江西南昌的滕王阁也是重阳登高胜地。滕王阁因唐代诗人王勃于重阳节时在阁上写出千古名文《滕王阁序》，更加闻名天下。重阳这一天，来自海内外的众多游客登上江南名楼滕王阁，欣赏赣江美景。而在滕王阁楼下，不少年过七旬的老人会在此耍太极，以此庆祝属于老年人自己的节日。

旅游小贴士

南昌滕王阁

滕王阁有"西江第一楼"之称，位于南昌市西北部沿江路赣江东岸，与湖北黄鹤楼、湖南岳阳楼并称为"江南三大名楼"。滕王阁在古代被人们看作是吉祥风水建筑，古人认为如果滕王阁和绳金塔倒塌，豫章城中的人才与宝藏都将流失，城市亦将败落，不复繁荣昌盛。在我国古代习俗中，人口聚居之地需要风水建筑，一般为当地最高标志性建筑，聚集天地之灵气，吸收日月之精华，俗称"文笔峰"。滕王阁坐落于赣水之滨，被古人誉为"水笔"。古人云："求财去万寿宫，求福去滕王阁"。可见滕王阁在世人心目中占据的神圣地位，在历朝历代无不备受重视和保护。同时，滕王阁也是古代储藏经史典籍的地方，从某种意义上来说是古代的图书馆。而封建士大夫们迎送和宴请宾客也多喜欢在此，贵为天子的明代开国皇帝朱元璋在鄱阳湖之战大胜陈友谅后，曾设宴阁上，命诸大臣、文人赋诗填词，观看灯火。

最佳旅游季节：3月~5月和9月~11月最佳。

地址：南昌市东湖区沿江北大道39号（近叠山路）

○滕王阁

　　关于登高，还有一个有趣的典故，叫作"孟嘉落帽"。孟嘉是东晋时代的著名文人。征西大将军桓温任江州刺史时，见孟嘉待人谦逊而正直，很是看重他，便任命他为参军。那年的九月初九重阳节，桓温带着属下的文武官员游览龙山，登高赏菊，并在山上设宴欢饮，桓温的四个弟弟和两位外甥都列席。当时大小官员都身着戎装。山上金风送爽，花香沁人心脾。突然一阵无头风扑面吹来，竟把孟嘉的帽子吹落在地,但他一点也没有察觉,仍举杯痛饮。因为古人把帽子看得和头颅一样重要,所以孟嘉落帽惊动了在座的宾客。桓温见了,暗暗称奇,以目示意,叫大家不要声张,看孟嘉有什么举动。但见孟嘉依然谈笑风生,浑然不觉。又过了很久,孟嘉起身离座去上厕所。桓温趁机让人把孟嘉的帽子捡起来,放在他的席位上。又命人取来纸笔,让当时著名的文人孙盛写了一张字条,嘲弄孟嘉落帽却不自知,有失体面。写好后让桓温过目,桓温觉得很有趣,想乘酒兴调侃奚落他一番。便把

○ 国画"孟嘉落帽图"

纸条压在帽子下。孟嘉回到座位时,才发觉自己落帽失礼。但却不动声色地顺手拿起帽子戴正。又拿起字条看了一遍,即请左右取来纸笔,不假思索,奋笔疾书,一气呵成一篇诙谐而文采四溢的答词,为自己的落帽失礼辩护。桓温和满座宾朋争相传阅,无不击掌叹服。

"孟嘉落帽"这个成语不单被用来形容才子名士的风雅洒脱、才思敏捷,还常被历代文人在重阳登高时引用。比如唐代诗人李白的《九日》中写道:"落帽醉山月,空歌怀友生。"

登高时候聊聊典故,也成为重阳节的一大乐趣。

（二）赏菊、喝菊花酒

赏菊、喝菊花酒，是重阳节的又一象征性活动。在中国，一提到菊花，大家似乎就习惯性地把它和重阳节联系在一起。中国人偏爱菊花，早在三千多

○重阳赏菊

年前人们就开始栽种菊花了。菊花在秋季开放，故为秋的象征。人们甚至把九月称"菊月"，因为菊与"据"同音，"九"又与"久"同音，"九"

○国画"松菊图"

是所有数字中最大的，所以菊花也被用来象征长寿或长久，并且认为农历九月初九重阳节这一天采的菊花更有意义，常用这天采到的菊花精制菊花茶，或者将这一天采的菊花泡陈年米酒，做成香醇的菊花酒，又或者是用菊花沐浴，皆取"菊水上寿"之意。

如果在一个画面上画有菊花和鹌鹑，因为"鹌"的发音与"安"相同，代表的是安乐、平安、安详，和菊花画在一起还有安居的意思。菊与松树画在一起，叫作"松菊延年"，表示祝愿接受此画的人长寿。还有人把一只蝈蝈儿画在菊花之上，因"蝈"与"官"

发音相近，即表示祝愿别人长久(九)占据官位,其画名为"官居一品"。

我国有饮菊花酒的传统习俗。菊花酒,在古代被看作是重阳必饮、祛灾祈福的"吉祥酒"。酿制菊花酒,早在汉魏时期就已盛行。《西京杂记》记载了菊花酒的做法:在九月九日这一天,采下初开的菊花瓣和嫩枝叶,撒入粮食中,封好坛子,待到来年重九日,再和亲友品菊花酒,吟诗作赋,互诉衷肠。果然,一有了美酒,古人就容易乱心动情,澎湃的诗意绵延不绝,滚滚而出,挡都挡不住。晋代诗人陶渊明也在诗作中写到饮菊花酒能祛百病,食菊花有延缓衰老的功效。后来饮菊花酒逐渐成了民间的

○国画"晋饮菊花酒"

○菊花酒

一种风俗习惯,尤其是在重阳时节,更要饮菊花酒。《荆楚岁时记》载称在九月九日这天佩茱萸,食莲饵,饮菊花酒,可以长寿。到了明清时期,菊花酒中又加入多种草药,养生效果更佳。

（三）放纸鹞

○纸鸢图案

九月九重阳节，除了登高、饮菊花酒、食重阳糕以外，还有一个重要的习俗，那就是放纸鹞。纸鹞又称为纸鸢，也就是我们现在所说的风筝，而纸鹞则是风筝最古老的称呼。据说，放纸鹞也来自恒景与费长房的传说。恒景当年在拜访仙长求除魔的途中得到了鸽子的指引，才找到了那个有着神奇法力的仙长费长房。后人为了纪念此事，就用纸糊出鸽子的形状，然后带到山上放飞，久而久之就演变成了放纸鹞的习俗。

○墨子

风筝最早的称呼叫"纸鹞"。五代以后才叫"风筝"。风筝起源于何时？由谁发明？对于这种问题的解释，众说纷纭。主要有以下几种说法。

一种说法是，风筝起源于先秦，由中国古代伟大的思想家、科学家、教育家、军事家和社会活动家墨子所做。传说墨子在鲁山研究试制了三年，终于用木板制成了一只木鸟，但只飞了一天就坏了。墨子制造的这只"木鹞"就是中国最早的风筝，也是世界上最早的风筝。（约公元前300年），距今已有两千四百年历史了。之后，墨子把制风筝的事业传给了他的学生鲁班，《墨子·鲁问篇》中说，鲁班根据墨子的理想和设计，用竹子做风筝。鲁班把竹子劈开削光滑，用火烤弯曲，做成了喜鹊的样子，称为"木鹊"，在空中飞翔达三天之久。当年墨子发明风筝的鲁山，就在现在山东潍坊境内。现在的潍坊，又被称作"鸢都"，即风筝的故乡。潍坊制作风筝历史悠久，工艺精湛，现在世界上70%以上的风筝都出自潍坊。2006年5月，潍坊风筝被列入第一批国家级非物质文化遗产名录。"国际风筝联合会"的总部也设定在潍坊。现在潍坊成为世界风筝文化交流的中心，被世界各国人民称为风筝的故乡。潍坊风筝同中国许多民间艺术形式一样，产生于人们的娱乐活动，寄托着人们的理想和愿望，是与人们的生活有密切联系的娱乐物品。

○潍坊国际风筝会

旅游小贴士

潍坊国际风筝会

潍坊风筝会于每年 4 月 20 日至 25 日在潍坊举行，有来自世界各地的 30 多个国家和地区的代表队参赛，是我国最早冠以"国际"并被国际社会承认的大型地方节会。从 1984 年至今，已成功举办过三十三届，其创立的"风筝牵线、文体搭台、经贸唱戏"的模式，被全国各地广为借鉴。潍坊是风筝的发祥地。1983 年 5 月，在上海举行的中国出口商品交易会上，潍坊工美应邀参加表演的 28 只潍坊风筝引起了国内外观众的注目。尤其是长达 50 米的龙头蜈蚣风筝，更令人连连称奇。当时，赴上海参加交易会的美国西雅图市风筝协会主席大卫·切克列先生对潍坊的风筝产生深刻的印象。会后，他专程来潍坊订购了一批风筝带回美国。也正是这次大卫·切克列与潍坊的亲密接触，把潍坊风筝推上国际舞台。

据不完全统计，每年风筝会期间，前来潍坊进行体育比赛、文艺演出、经贸洽谈、观光旅游、对外交流、理论研讨、新闻报道、文化交流等活动的国内外宾客近 60 万人。

时间：每年 4 月 20 日至 25 日都会举办潍坊国际风筝会。

地址：潍坊市位于山东半岛。距离省会济南路程约 213.3 千米。可乘坐大巴、火车到达。

还有一种说法，风筝是中国汉初伟大的军事家、战略家韩信发

多彩中国节

重阳节

明的。唐朝赵昕写的《息灯鹞文》一书中说，项羽和刘邦原来约定以鸿沟（在今河南荥县境内贾鲁河）东西边作为界限，互不侵犯。后来刘邦听从张良和陈平的规劝，觉得应该趁项羽衰弱的时候消灭他，就又和韩信等追击项羽部队。终于布置了几层兵力，把项羽部队团团围住。这时，项羽手下的兵士已经很少，粮食又没有了。刘邦不想硬拼而想瓦解敌军，这时韩信就建议扎制大风筝、绑上哨子升上空中，哨子会在空中响起来，形成天上"四面楚歌"，让项羽以为楚地已经被征服。这个建议受到刘邦的赞赏。于是韩信设计出风筝雏形，并找来了一位住在楚地南通的吴姓木匠师傅合力完成第一只风筝，吴师傅又将三只大小不同的竹哨连成一组，固定在风筝的骨架上。风筝试飞成功后，韩信便号召营中所有懂得手工技艺的士兵们一起投入扎制风筝，大家各显其能，又用果壳制哨、葫芦制成哨子，军营变成了历史上第一座风筝工坊。

○放风筝

夜里将风筝放入空中，清脆的哨音从天而降，音调不同、高低不等、如歌似曲、如泣如诉。身处楚国军营中的兵士，被天上、地面的楚歌搞得草木皆兵，项羽也被连日来的楚地山歌所误导，最终失败。

唐朝以后，作为军事用途的纸鸢开始向民间娱乐转化，成为年轻人、儿童的嬉耍物品。到宋代，放风筝已成为流行于民间的娱乐活动和喜事的庆祝纪念活动。由于风筝的普及，当时放风筝已成为一种技艺。逢庙会、集市、节日和游戏时，都有人表演制作和放风筝。南宋末，开始出现以扎售风筝为业的手工艺人。

放风筝是重阳节的重要娱乐活动，南北方都有，尤其在南方盛行。重阳节前后的南方秋高气爽，且季风渐强。重阳节这天，人们按照习俗要登山、登高，扶老携幼到户外郊游，此时放风筝就显得十分适宜。

○扶老携幼放风筝

放风筝被赋予了许多含义，主要体现在两个方面，一个是"送吉祥"，另一个是"放晦气"。

先说说"送吉祥"。放风筝不止是一种娱乐活动，它还被民众赋予了祈福、祝愿的意义。在一些地方，放风筝前要举行隆重的仪式，在村头摆设香案，村民们一起祈求风调雨顺、五谷丰登。

传统的中国风筝上到处可见带有吉祥寓意的图案。在漫长的岁月里，我们的祖先不仅创造出优美的凝聚着中华民族智慧的文字和绘画，还创造了许多反映人们对美好生活向往和追求、寓意吉祥的图案。它通过图案形象，给人以喜庆、吉祥如意和祝福之意。它融合了群众的审美习惯，反映人们善良健康的思想感情，渗透着我国民族传统和民间习俗，因而在民间广泛流传，为人们喜闻乐见。

传统的风筝上有许多象征吉祥寓意的图案。比如在南方，以蝙蝠为图案的风筝比比皆是。蝙蝠的发音与"遍福""遍富"的发音相近，于是它就成为了象征"福气"的吉祥图案。其他的求福图案还有鱼和如意，寓意为"富余"和"尽如人意"。

除此以外，龙、凤、麒麟也是中国人心目中的瑞禽瑞兽。龙是中华民族的象征，是千百年来黎民百姓崇拜的偶像，所以中国人也称自己为龙的传人；凤被称为鸟中之王；麒麟是古代传说中的一种神兽，古人以它象征吉祥。

○蝙蝠风筝

与"送吉祥"风俗相反的是"放晦气"。放风筝一开始和原始宗教活动密切相关。在过去还长期处于生产力水平十分低下，科学技术极不发达的时代，人们没有能力抵御疾病以及各种自然灾害的侵袭，更不明白造成人类痛苦贫困的社会根源，因此产生了崇拜神灵、祈求天赐好运的心理。这种信仰表现在各个方面，在放风筝上也有所寄托。人们在风筝上写上自己的名字，然后放上天去，又故意剪断牵线，让风筝飞走。认为这样就可放走"晦气"，交上好运，达成"消灾祛难"的愿望。

因此，在放风筝时，不管风筝如何玲珑好看，最后都必须剪断牵线，让它飞走，同时，又产生了忌讳习俗，即人家放掉的风筝，不能拾来重放，否则会染上"晦气"。这种风俗，在民间又叫"放断鹞"。

"放晦气"的风俗，不仅我国有，国外也有。如我国的邻邦朝鲜在每年风筝节中，人们把自己的苦恼——写在纸做的飘带上，然后缚在风筝上。当风筝飞上天空后，他们就把放风筝的绳子割断，风筝随风飞走了。人们认为自己的苦恼也随之消失了。

在潮汕农村，有不少人信深信，认为农历九月九日"重阳节"是"转运日"。在此日有些人携带自己的风筝登高放飞，意谓"衰运"尽去，"好运"将来。人人都想方设法让自己的风筝顺利高飞并任其飞走，以偿心愿。不过有不少风筝在中途放飞时断线，故当地民间谚语曰："九月九，风筝断线满天走。"对断线飞来的风筝，忌捡，怕捡到别人的"衰运"。

○放风筝 放走晦气

在福州，捡断线风筝到底晦不晦气，没有一个准确说法，但是福州人重阳登高放风筝，最忌讳的就是"风筝断线"，连提到这几个字都是不被允许的。"断线风筝"不吉利。意味着有不好的事会发生。过去人们嫁女儿，刚过门或还没进门，女婿就死了或毁婚，就叫"断线"，可见对风筝线断了这件事，人们很忌讳。

放纸鹞是惠州过重阳节的主要习俗。换句话说，惠州民间过重阳节是以放纸鹞为主要特征的。此习俗，除惠州流传的民谣中有叙述以外，光绪年间《惠州府志》亦有记述。而现在惠州民间的纸鹞，已非本来面目，多为四方平面，带一尾巴，其形状与民间所贴门神、神位相似，故疑为神状风筝的一种简化。在惠州民间，风筝制作极为简单，采竹，一支弯曲，一支直竖，撑住一张四方形纸，贴上尾巴调好线，即可放飞。有一种不带尾巴，四方形纸稍大，称"阿婆鹞"，以放飞时平稳而得名。

（四）祭扫祖墓，纪念先人

重阳节与除、清、盂三节共同成为中国传统节日里祭祖的四大节日。重阳扫墓祭祖也颇有渊源。重阳节早在战国时期就已经形成，到了唐代，重阳被正式定为民间的节日，旧时按惯例这天所有亲人都要一起登高"避灾"。至今，在浙江桐庐、福建莆仙及台湾、新加坡等不少地方，人们在九月九日仍"备猪羊以祭祖"，称为秋祭。据了解，如今珠三角的孔子后裔，每年重阳也会到广州白云区的凤鸣古冢祭祖——拜太公，是为家传古风。在福建莆仙，当地人也会利用重阳登山的机会，祭扫祖墓，纪念先人。莆仙人因重阳祭祖者比清明多，故俗有"三月为小清明，重九为大清明"之说。同时，由于莆仙沿海，九月九也是妈祖羽化升天的忌日，乡民多到湄洲妈祖庙或港里的天后祖祠、宫庙祭祀，求妈祖保佑。总之，每逢佳节倍思亲。

福州的重阳节，还有祭扫祖坟的活动，这与清明的祭坟，合称春秋二祭。现在福州的郊区或郊县，仍保留九月九扫墓的习俗。

重阳扫墓，切合山区实际，大有好处。因为山区的墓葬大多位于山边、岭上，周边基本上是草木丛生，清明时节雨纷纷，行走多有不便，爬山越岭扫墓难免把衣衫都弄湿了。重阳则不同，正是秋高气爽之时，雨水偏少，这时扫墓不仅出行方便，还可登高远眺，欣赏各处美景。况且，重阳节一般与国庆节相距很近，这时外出工作的人也容易安排时间回乡与亲人一起扫墓祭祖。这些扫墓人士大多以一个或数个家庭为单位，带上丰富的祭品和香烛来拜祭先人。许多香港人扫完墓、看望过先人之后，再举家带上吃喝，去野外郊游。所以清晨去墓地的公路特别拥挤。

II

The Traditions of the Double Ninth Festival

People hold various interesting and entertaining activities to celebrate the Double Ninth Festival when the golden autumn season brings about pleasant coolness and osmanthus blooms fragrantly. The Double Ninth Festival, shaped by thousands of years' cultural screening and depositing, inherited the traditions of having Double Ninth Cake, wearing zhuyu, appreciationg Chrysanthemum, climbing mountains, flying kites, and paying homage to ancestors, etc.

1. The Food Customs of the Double Ninth Festival

1.1 Having Double Ninth Cake

Having Double Ninth Cake (The Chinese character for cake is 糕 which has the same pronunciation gao with 高 which means height) is the representative tradition of spending the Double Ninth Festival.

The Double Ninth Cake is made of steamed rice flour used for treating guests and offering sacrifices. It is called flower cake, chrysanthemum cake, or five-colored cake, depending on the different ways of making it. In ancient China, it was held that a country's prosperity depended on agriculture's development. For celebrating harvest, people would make rice cakes to present to their relatives and friends before and after the Double Ninth Festival. They stuck colorful mini-flags into the steamed cakes, dotted with pomegranate seeds, chestnuts, or pine nuts. The Double Ninth Cake, named Steamed Cake today, tastes soft, sweet, and sticky. It's very delicious.

The tradition of having the Double Ninth Cake can date back to very early period. In the Han Dynasty, it was called Er, a kind of steamed cake made of rice and millet flour, the latter being sticky. The millet was a very important kind of grains of the ancient Chinese people used for treating guests and offering sacrifices. In Sept. after the millet got ripe, people would pay homage to ancestors by it to show their respect because it was the newly-harvested crop. The Double Ninth Cake we have today originates from the newly-harvested food. This is also the

Double Ninth Cake Beautifully Decorated

origin of today's autumn sacrifices to deities and ancestors.

It was about in the Song Dynasty that the tradition of having the Double Ninth Cake had been officially recorded; for example, a man of letter in the Song Dynasty, Wu Zimu, wrote in his work *Annals of Lin'an City in Dream* (Lin'an is the capital city of the Southern Song Dynasty; today's Hangzhou City), "On the Double Ninth day, people steam cakes by using sweet rice flour ... dotted with small colored flags, named the Double Ninth Cake." The tradition of decorating the cakes with small colored flags has been carried onto today.

People in different regions will make the Double Ninth Cake in different ways. All of the soft and sweet cakes made on the Double Ninth Day are called the Double Ninth Cake.

Because cake has the same pronunciation with height, and having it means being promoted, people extremely favored it. Those people who're particular about it will make nine-layered cake, looking like a pagoda and symbolizing nine-layered heaven while some people will decorate the cake with five colors—red, black, yellow, white, and green because the ancient Chinese people believed that the five colors on the earth could drive away the evil spirits and they were very superstitious about their functions. So they not only had the cakes themselves but also presented them to their relatives and friends.

On the Double Ninth Festival, there was another tradition, fetching the married daughters home, named Guining (meaning returning home and enjoying peaceful days). According to *A Brief Sketch of the Capital Scenes* written at the end of the Ming Dynasty, parents must fetch their married daughters home for having the Double Ninth Cake; otherwise, the parents would be scolded. That's why this festival is called Daughters' Day.

There're two sayings about having the Double Ninth Cake: one is that before the Emperor Gaozu, Liu Yu, captivated the sovereignty of the Jin Dynasty, he had the Double Ninth Festival in Pengcheng City. Out of impulse, he climbed onto the Horsemanship Terrace built by Xiang Yu , the monarch of the West Chu Kingdom. After he succeeded in throne, he stipulated that every Sept. 9th was the day for horse-riding, shooting and viewing troops. Today's Double Ninth Cake is originally the solid food for the soldiers.

Tourist tips

Xuzhou Horsemanship Terrace

The Xuzhou Horsemanship Terrace, located on the top of the Hubu Mountain in downtown of Xuzhou City, Jiangsu Province, is originally the most well-known historical interest there. In 206 B.C., Xiang Yu, the hero of the age, claimed to be the West Chu Kingdom Supreme Ruler, set his capital in Pengcheng City (today's Xuzhou). On the top of the South Mountain in the south of the city, he built the Horsemanship Terrace for horsemanship, military drill, and viewing troops.

Address: 1 Xiangwang Road, Yun Long District, Xuzhou City, Jiangsu Province

Another saying is popular in Shanxi Province. The tale goes like this: Kanghai, a *Zhuangyuan* (champion in the imperial examination of recruiting officials), born in Wugong, Shanxi Province, got sick after the examination and had to stay in Chang'an (the capital city of the Tang Dynasty, today's Xi'an City) for recovery. After the examination result was released, the messenger sent this good news to Kang's hometown, but Kang was still in Chang'an. So nobody could award the messenger gratuity. He insisted on waiting for Kang's return. When Kang went back home, it was the Double Ninth Festival. He gave the messenger gratuity and a bag of steamed rice cakes as solid food. He also sent the cakes to his neighbors for celebrating this happy event. Therefore, those families who had children in school would distribute the cakes on the Double Ninth day for seeking fortune: Gradually Rising to Eminence (*Bu Bu Gao Sheng*).

Besides having the cakes themselves, people also presented the cakes to their relatives and friends, named *songgao*, meaning bringing about fortune. The tradition of having Double Ninth Cake has been observed by the Chinese people for several thousands of years for the purpose of praying for peace and health. It's most prominent in Beijing, Shanxi Province, and Shandong Province.

In the old Beijing, there were great varieties of flower cakes. One are the roast cakes and pastries sold in the pastry shops, such as *caozi gao* (cake), *taoshu*(walnut cake), *wangao*(bowl cake), and *saqima* (candied fritter), etc.; another kind of is

Villagers in Liaocheng City, Shandong Province Making Double Ninth Flower Cakes

the Gold and Silver Honeycomb Cake, steamed rice and millet flour cake, made by the housewives living in the closed courtyards or the women farmers, dotted with peanuts, almond, pine nuts, walnuts, and sunflower seeds. Others are steamed rice flour cake with fat, five-colored cake with flour dyed, cake mixed with jujube, sweet, raisins, and dried fruits, or sprinkled with pork shreds, chicken and duck shreds and decorated with the Chinese characters *Jixiang* ("吉祥" meaning good luck) or *Fu Shou Lu Xi* ("福寿禄禧" respectively meaning blessing, longevity, promotion, and happiness), as well as ornamented with five-colored flags. People bought the flower cakes home and exhibited them in the Buddha Hall, Ancestral Hall, or presented to their relatives or friends as gifts.

In Shanxi Province, besides presenting flower cakes, people do *Qulian*, too. The former one is steamed while the latter is roast by ao. The former, always being circular or oval, has three to seven layers, with the implication of gradually rising to height. Each layer of cakes is decorated with flowers on top of the cakes, various kinds of flowers blossom, being aesthetically appealing. These are called flower cakes. Qulian ("曲连" meaning being cursive and linked to each other), the latter, are roast cakes, with varieties of patterns, such as jade ring, sickle, and axe, etc., which are cursively linked to each other, hence the name.

People send flower cakes or Qulian in the following way: a big flower cake or Qulian matched with several small ones;

except from the big ones, smaller ones must be presented in even number; two or four small ones will be presented to the family with only one child while six or eight small ones to the family with two children. And the small flower cakes can also be called *Shuagao* ("耍糕" meaning cake for playing by children).

Tool for Making Qulian: *Ao* (Qulian Roaster)

In Shandong Province, the flower cake is made of steamed flour, mixed with jujube and chestnut, etc., or decorated with colored paper flags, called flower cake flag. Some of the cakes are ornamented with two flour-molded sheep ("羊" with the same pronunciation as "阳" *yang*)for the auspicious implication of duplicate *yang* in the Chongyang Festival, the Double Ninth Festival. The flower cakes are festival food and gifts. In the north of Jinan City, Shandong Province, people present not only cakes but also clothes for autumn and winter.

1.2 Having rice jelly and crab roe

In Puxian of Fujian Province, people observe the tradition of steaming nine-layered rice cake, or so-called Er by the ancient Chinese people. Song Zuqian, a local poet in the beginning of the Qing Dynasty, wrote *Fujian Wine Melody*:

"The Double Ninth Festival is coming soon,

The girls pick wild greens with slender hands;

Pounded by the jade pestle into green paste wet with rice,

Sweet heart, please hurry and taste the emerald-like cakes."

In the modern era, people adapted the traditional rice cake into a nine-layered one. Here's the recipe: rinse the quality rice

Nine-Layered Jelly

and immerse it for two hours, drain it, grind it with water into syrup, add alum (dissolved with water) and stir it, add caramel (simmering brown sugar into thick syrup), put the steamer on the stove, spread a kitchen cloth in the steamer, scoop the rice syrup on the kitchen cloth layer by layer for nine times, steam it, open the steamer, smear some peanut oil onto the cake, and cut it into cubes. It can be cut into the shape of diamond, too. The nine-layered rice cake, being translucent, soft, sweet, and glutinous, but not sticky onto the teeth, is truly the best gift for the elderly on the Double Ninth Festival. People in Fuzhou City, the capital city of Fujian Province, also make special dessert, Jiuchong Ke, a kind of nine-layered jelly, seven layers being caramel, with the implication of Rising to Height Step by Step and driving away disasters by height ascending.

In Yangzhou City of Jiangsu Province, having the Double Ninth Cake is a seasonal must. The shape of the cake is generally square, small and cute, dyed with red dots on the top. The cake hawker stacks the small cubes of cake and stuck onto them small red or green triangular flags, with many small holes pricked into them. The pricked paper flags become supple and can flutter in the breeze. These are so-called Double Ninth Flag. In the old times, the Double Ninth Cake is more exquisite than that of today. Li Xiufang (1793—1867), a writer in the Qing Dynasty, mentioned in his work, *The Preface to Collections of Ci with Bamboo Tune—the Annals of Zhenzhou* (today's Yizheng city of Jiangsu Province), a rice cake shop named Beauty Xiao, which sold Beauty Xiao Rice Cake, a local specialty during that time, every Double Ninth Festival, the origin of today's Double Ninth Cake. This book also recorded the ways of making the Double Ninth Cake, such as putting red or green Double Ninth Flags, molding miniature pavilions, sheep which are both delicious and aesthetically appealing.

In the south of the Qin Lin Mountains and Huaihe River, there're numerous rivers and lakes which constitute the vast water area. On the Double Ninth Festival in the gold autumn when the chrysanthemum blooms fragrantly, the ripe freshwater crabs are tender and rich in roe. It's the best season to have them. It's the same case in Xuzhou City of Jiangsu Province. The tale says that as early as in the West Zhou Dynasty, there was crab sauce. In the Tang and Song Dynasty, scalded crabs were very popular. The ancient Chinese people often exclaimed, "If you don't visit the Lushan Mountain, your eyes won't be pleased; if you don't have crabs, your palate won't be satisfied."

The autumn crabs are delicious, esp. the Yangcheng Lake crabs in Jiangsu Province. The restaurants will promote specialties made of crabs. The Steamed Yangcheng Lake Crabs, well-known at home and abroad, are September specialty in Hong Kong, Macao, Taiwan restaurants. Another kind of brand-crab of Jiangsu Province is produced in the Weishan Lake near Xuzhou City. People in Xuzhou feast on crabs when they spend the Mid-Autumn Festival and the Double Ninth

Festival because they're the best match with chrysanthemum wine. Many families are afraid that big crabs are not available on the Double Ninth Festival and will buy them in advance. They will bind the crabs with fine threads or wrap them up with rush-woven packets, sprinkle water onto them to keep them wet, which can make them alive and fresh in a short time. You'd better bind the crabs' legs and pincers tightly which will be otherwise kicked off if the crabs struggle with each other. In this way, there will be only shells left, which will spoil the intactness of the Steamed Crabs. As for the seasonings, because, according to the traditional Chinese medicine, crab is of cold nature, it's necessary to apply minced ginger, rice vinegar, and a little bit of sugar to neutralize the cold nature and bring out its original flavor. Imagine that you enjoy the tender and fresh crab while drinking the fine chrysanthemum wine, chatting with your family members or friends! What a strong festive aroma!

The tradition of having crabs also prevails in Shaoxing, Zhejiang Province, a region of rivers and lakes, where crabs abound. There's such folk saying here: Spiral shells on the Tomb Sweeping Festival, shrimps on the Dragon Boat Festival, and crabs on the Double Ninth Festival. The Shaoxing people call crabs *hengpa* (横爬 horizontally crawling) in a humorous way.

2. The Wearing Traditions of the Double Ninth Festival

There's one tradition which is closely related to height ascending, i.e., wearing *zhuyu*, among the many ones of the Double Ninth Festival. Zhuyu is a kind of small deciduous tree with mini-yellow flowers. It's ripe in autumn with red, oval fruits. It's a kind of evergreen, fragrant plant, whose tubers, leaves, and fruits can be used for traditional Chinese medicine with the functions of killing pests, sterilization, driving away the coldness, and relieving rheumatic pains. The ancient Chinese people used it for treating cholera. *The Compendium of Materia Medica* said that *zhuyu*, being spicy, pungent, and fragrant, is of warm nature, and can be used for driving away the coldness and getting rid of poison in the body.

The original name of *zhuyu* was *Wuyu* since it grew in the Wu Kingdom before the Qin Dynasty (221 B.C.—207 B.C.).

Wu zhuyu (*zhuyu* growing in today's Jiangsu Province)

It acquired the current name *zhuyu* owing to the following story:

In the Spring and Autumn and the Warring States Periods, the weak Wu Kingdom had to pay tribute to its powerful neighbor, the Chu Kingdom, annually. One year, the envoy of the Wu Kingdom dedicated Wu's specialty, *wuyu*, as a kind of medicine to the Chu King, who loved pearls, emeralds, gold, and silver so much that he looked down upon this humble plant. So, he suspected that the envoy was teasing him, burst into anger, and commanded to have the envoy driven away from the kingdom without listening to the latter's defense.

There was a doctor whose surname was Zhu in the Chu court had a close association with the Wu envoy, brought the latter home, and comforted him. The Wu envoy told him that *zhuyu* was the quality herbal medicine in his country with the function of warming stomach, stopping vomiting, and treating stomachache and diarrhea. Because he knew that the Chu King had suffered from stomachache caused by the coldness, he dedicated *wuyu* to him. He did not expect that the Chu King would treat him in such a rude way. ... As a result, Doctor Zhu sent the Wu envoy back to his country and kept the plant cautiously.

The next year, the Chu King suffered from a severe stomachache caused by coldness while the doctors had no way to treat it. Dr. Zhu caught this opportunity, simmered *wuyu* with water, and sent it to the king. Shortly after, pain was killed

Wearing Zhuyu

and the king was so ecstatic that he decided to award Dr. Zhu and asked what kind of medicine it was. Dr. Zhu retold the story of the Wu envoy. The Chu King was so regretful that he dispatched people to the Wu Kingdom, presented gifts to the Wu King, and apologized to him. After that, he ordered to have *wuyu* planted in the Chu Kingdom.

Several years later, the plague struck the Chu Kingdom. Hundreds of thousands of people who suffered from stomachache were saved by taking *zhuyu*. The Chu people inserted one word *zhu* between *wu* and *yu*, hence the name *wu zhu yu*, which was carried on unto today. Due to its special medicinal function, the ancient Chinese people were convinced that *zhuyu* could drive away the evil spirits and disasters.

There're varieties of ways for wearing Zhuyu. Some put it onto the head; some put it into the red fragrance sachet and bound it around the arm. *The Record of Local Customs* written by Zhou Chu of the Jin Dynasty (265 A.D.—420 A.D.) wrote, "It's customary for people to pick *zhuyu* fruits and wear them on the head in September for letting out the foul air in one's body and guarding against the coldness". It can be seen that the tradition of wearing *zhuyu* on the head had been observed for a long time.

The Collection of Monstrous and Mysterious Stories, Continued written by Wu Jun of the Southern Dynasty recorded the tales about the Double Ninth Festival mentioning wearing *zhuyu*. In Runan County, today's Shangcai County of Henan Province, a man named Huan Jing learnt Taoism from the immortal Fei Zhangfang. One day, Fei said to Huan that a great disaster would fall on his family on Sept. 9th and the only solution was putting *zhuyu* into a red sack and binding it round the arm, climbing to the top of mountain, drinking some chrysanthemum wine, and going back home after the dusk. On that day, Huan followed his master's words. After they went back home after the dusk, cattle, sheep, chickens, and dogs were found dead. Wearing *zhuyu* helped his family avoid the disaster. This is the origin of wearing *zhuyu*. So *zhuyu* is also called Avoiding Disaster Old Man.

Red Sachet for *zhuyu*, as a kind of folk craft, has become a logo of the Double Ninth Festival. Shangcai County, Henan Province, as the source of the sachet, carries on and promotes the tradition. In 2006, the Red Sachet for Zhuyu made by Zhang She, an elderly lady, attended the National Craft

Exhibition in Shenzhen City of Guangdong Province. In the same year, the Henan Provincial Government included it on the list of the first batch of provincial intangible cultural heritages.

Background information

Zhang She, the old lady in the above picture, 85 years old, is the inheritor of the intangible cultural heritage of Henan Province. She can make more than forty kinds of Red Sachet for *zhuyu* with lively patterns true to life. In the meanwhile, she was devoted to spreading the crafts and more than forty folk artists have become her disciples.

The tradition of wearing *zhuyu* in different ways reflected the aspiration of the ordinary people to extricate themselves from diseases and disasters. Therefore, people wear *zhuyu* on the head or bind it on the arm for driving away the evil and disaster. People in some places cut colored silk into the shape of *zhuyu* and chrysanthemum and present to each other. Wearing *zhuyu*, above all, demonstrates people's wish for health and peace.

3. The Folk Customs of the Double Ninth Festival

The Double Ninth Festival is a traditional Chinese one which integrates various kinds of folk customs. Around the ninth day of the ninth month of the Chinese lunar calendar, when the gold autumn brings about the cool breeze and the golden osmanthus blooms, people celebrate the Double Ninth Festival in many ways, including going out for sceneries, climbing mountains, enjoying chrysanthemums while drinking the chrysanthemum wine, wearing Zhuyu, having the Double Ninth Cake, and sweeping the tombs for worshipping the ancestors, etc.

3.1 Ascending a height

Ascending a Height is one of the major customs on the Double Ninth Festival. In ancient China, the festival had got an additional name "Height Ascending Festival" due to this custom. On this golden autumn day, the whole family get together, climb to the top of the mountain, indulge themselves in the beautiful sceneries of the autumn when the yellow chrysanthemums are at their prime. It was recorded that the custom of height ascending originated from the Eastern Han Dynasty and reached its peak in the Tang Dynasty when a lot of poets wrote poems for the festival, among which, Height Ascending by Tu Fu and the Ninth Day by Cui Guofu were household ones. Owing to the custom of height ascending, the distant travelers have the chance of looking far into their hometown; thus, this festival bears the color of homesickness.

The custom of Ascending a Height has a long history. There're about three kinds of sayings about its origin. One is for escaping disasters and evils; another demonstrating the ancient people's worshipping for mountains; and the third is to say goodbye to the green summer, a counterpart of Spring Hiking in the third month of the Chinese lunar calendar since the Double Ninth Festival is in the autumn season after which the plants will wither day by day.

As a matter of fact, the custom of Climbing the Mountain is closely related to the essential subsistence need of the early human beings. In the ancient times, people, living in caves and forests, fed on hunting animals and gathering fruits of plants. Their survival mainly relied on mountain forests. When it was hot, the earth being scorched by the sun, people would hide themselves in the mountain forest; when it was cold, people

Wu Ta (Five-Pagoda) Temple

would do so, too, because thunder and flash on the top of the mountain would cause fire which would bring about warmness and brightness and be used for cooking. Using fire distinguished human beings from animals. When it was flooding, people climbed onto the mountain for escaping disasters. The high mountains were covered in thick mists and clouds,

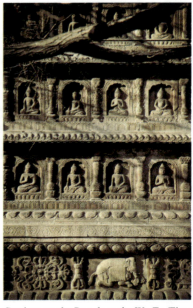

Carvings on the Pagoda at the Wu Ta (Five-Pagoda) Temple

causing rain, which made the ancient people believe that there were immortals living there with the power of generating rain. In the meanwhile, the towering peaks were thought to be ladders, on which, the ancient people believed that they could step to heaven and become immortals, too. The volatile natural phenomena, breeding the ancient people's belief that everything under the heaven had a spirit, and thus their worshipping the mountain, inspired their awe for Height and aroused their strong will for ascending the Height and becoming immortals. Some scholars held that the Chinese character 崇 , composed of 山 (mountain)and 宗 (showing respect for), literally means worshipping the mountain.

From the Qin Dynasty when China was united to the Han Dynasty (206 B.C.—260 A.D.), the emperors were keen of offering sacrifices to mountains and rivers. They annually went for inspection and hunting tours and offered sacrifices to famous mountains and rivers. According to history, at the end of the Qin Dynasty, the South Yue (located in today's Guangdong and Guangxi Provinces) King, Zhao Tuo, set the capital in Panyu (today's Guangzhou), had climbed onto the Yuexiu Mountain with his officials. The Min Yue King of the West Han Dynasty, Wuzhu, climbed onto the Yu Mountain (located in today's Fuzhou City), drank the chrysanthemum wine with his officials. So the Yu Mountain is also called the Ninth Day Mountain. These recordings are more than 200 years earlier that the aforementioned story "Huan Jing Defeating the Plague Monster".

The autumn is the best season for climbing mountain when it's cool, and the yellow chrysanthemum blooms. It's a great pleasure for family members get together and ascend the height by carrying fine wine and wearing *zhuyu*.

The old Beijing people were also fond of climbing the mountain on the Double Ninth Festival. The emperors, on the Double Ninth day, would climb on the top of the Longevity Mountain (today's Jingshan Mountain) for praying for blessings, longevity, and peace, as well as touring the scenery of Beijing while the empresses and concubines climbed to the top of the Duixiushan Mountain (Mountain of Stacked Embroidery) in the imperial garden for an overview of Beijing. The Empress Dowager Cixi of the Qing Dynasty climbed the Peach Blossom Mountain, east of Beihai Park, for picnic and barbeque while a blue cloth curtain would be set up from being peeped. The officials, men of letters or the ordinary people would climb to the top of the mountains, pavilions, towers, and terraces in their own gardens, or chose a mountain inside or outside Beijing for ascending the height and looking into distance. The latter would mainly go to the Xiangshan Mountain (Fragrance Mountain), the Wu Ta (Five-Pagoda) Temple, and the Jingshan Mountain Park with their families or friends. Nowadays, the Bejing people will tour the Xiangshan Mountain, Hong Luo Mountain (Red Spiral Snail Mountain),

Peonies at the Jingshan Mountain Park

or Baihua Mountain (Hundred Flower Mountain), with lush forestation and beautiful natural sceneries for spending the Double Ninth Festival.

Tourist tips

The Xiangshan Mountain (Fragrance Mountain) in Beijing

The Xiangshan Mountain (Fragrance Mountain), located in the west suburb of the Haidian District of Beijing, 25 km away from Beijing, with its summit, the Xianglu Peak (Incense Burner Peak), 575 meters above the sea level, is the well−known forest park in Beijing. In 2012, it was awarded the title of the Famous Mountain in the world, the fifth included on the list of the world−famous mountains after Mount Tai, the Huangshan Mountain, the Lushan Mountain, and the Er'mei Mountain. The Xiangshan Mounatain features its stunning beauty of Red Leaf Scenery, which was included to the list of the Sixteen New Scenic Spots of Beijing. In the deep autumn season, the leaves of the trees, with brilliant hues of red, give a flaming tribute to the mountain.

The best time: Sept. to Oct. when the frost strikes the trees and the whole mountain is covered in dazzling red;

Open: 06:00—18:30

Address: the east of the Xiaoxishan Mountain, north−west suburb of Haidian District of Beijing

The Tengwang Tower built by Li Yuanying, one of the younger brothers of the Emperor Taizong of the Tang Dynasty (618 A.D. to 907 A.D.), with the title of the King of Teng, is a scenic resort for ascending the height. This tower is famous for the masterpiece prose *The Preface to the Tengwang Tower* written

Octagonal Zaojing (ceiling decorated with painted engravings)

by the famous talented poet Wangbo in the Tang Dynasty. On the Double Ninth day, numerous tourists at home and abroad will climb onto the top of the Tengwang Tower for overlooking the Ganjiang River. And in front of the Tower, quite a number of elderly people over 70s will play *taiji* here for celebrating the Seniors' Day.

> ### Tourist tips
>
> ## The Tengwang Tower in Nanchang
>
> The Tengwang Tower, crowned as the First Tower in Jiangxi Province, located on the east bank of the Riverside Road, north-west of Nanchang City, is one of the three famous towers in China along with the Yellow Crane Tower in Hubei Province and the Yueyang Tower in Hunan Province. In ancient times, the Tower was deemed as architecture

of fengshui, the collapse of which, would cause the drain of the talents and treasures in Nanchang City and the ruin of this city accordingly. As a kind of ancient folk customs, it was routine to build architecture of fengshui in the place where people gathered, generally the tallest one there, which was thought to be able to absorb the essence of the heaven and the earth as well as that of the sun and the moon. The Tengwang Tower is located by the riverside of the Ganjiang River, was popularly known as the Wenbi (文 笔, in Chinese, meaning a literati) Peak. The old saying goes like "Go to the Longevity Palace for blessings; go to the Tengwang Tower for inspiration", which indicates the sacred position of the Tower in people's mind. Therefore, it had been protected by all dynasties and reigns. In the meanwhile, this Tower served as an ancient library for collecting and storing classical Chinese literature and classic works. On the other hand, the ancient men of letters and officials treated guests here. The first emperor of the Ming Dynasty, Zhu Yuanzhang, had ever hosted a banquet in honor of his officials and men of letters here, writing poems and watching fireworks, after defeating Chen Youliang, a powerful rival of his at the Poyanghu Lake, one of the four biggest lakes in China.

The best time: Mar. to May and Sept. to Nov.

Address: 39 North Riverside Road (Jindieshan Road), East Lake District, Nanchang City

There's another allusion related to Ascending the Height, that is, *Mengjia Dropping his Hat*. Mengjia was a well-known literati in the East Jin Dynasty. When Huan Wen, the General of Conquering the West, took the position of the Jiangzhou Governor, finding Meng was modest and righteous, and appointed him as the military staff officer. On the Double Ninth Festival of that year, Huan toured the Dragon Mountain with his subjects and his four younger brothers and nephews while enjoying chrysanthemums, and hosted a banquet. At that moment, all of the officials were dressed in military uniforms when suddenly a fit of wind blew off Meng's hat; however, he did not notice it at all and kept on drinking. Anyway, the ancient Chinese people took their hats as important as their heads, so all the other people present were shocked. Huan was so curious what Meng would do that he winked to the other people, not making a fuss. Nevertheless, Meng kept on talking and was not aware of it, yet. After a long time, Meng went to wash his hands. Huan took this opportunity to have Meng's hat picked up and put it on his table. Then he had paper and brush fetched and let Sunsheng, another famous literati, write a slip mocking Meng's indecent behavior. Huan thought it was a great fun and wanted to jeer at Meng. So he hid the slip under the hat. After Meng came back to his seat, he was aware of his indecent behavior, but he kept his countenance, wore his hat well, and wrote a humorous prose with literary grace to defend his behavior. His writing was passed on from one to another and was greatly applauded. Later, the allusion Mengjia Dropping His Hat was not only applied for describing the inhibited and wild nature as well as the intellect and wit of the men of letters but also for the occasion of the Double Ninth Festival; for example, Li Bai, the famous poet of the Tang Dynasty, had ever exclaimed in his *Ninth Day*,

"I was drunk with wine and the moon in the mountain,

Let the wind blow off my hat.

I sang and danced alone,

Wandering where my friends drifted."

It is a great pleasure to refer to the allusions about the Double Ninth Festival when ascending the height.

3.2 Enjoying Chrysanthemums and drinking chrysanthemum wine

Enjoying chrysanthemums and drinking chrysanthemum wine are another two symbolic customs of the Double Ninth Festival. In China, chrysanthemum has been closely associated with the festival. The Chinese people have been favoring chrysanthemum and began to plant it more than 3000 years ago. The chrysanthemum blooms in autumn, hence the symbol of this season. Chinese people even called Sept. (九月)the Chrysanthemum Month (菊月，in Chinese, the former character is homonymous

Enjoying Chrysanthemums

with 据 ,which means holding). And 九 is homonymous with 久 (meaning forever). As a result, Chinese people thought chrysanthemum was symbolic for longevity or eternity and the chrysanthemum picked on the Double Ninth day was more precious. They would use it for making tea or rice wine, or use it for bathing, hoping it would bring about health and longevity for them.

According to the Chinese traditions, if chrysanthemum is painted with a quail, the painting implies safety and peace since " 鹌 " (an) in " 鹌鹑 " (*anchun*; quail)is homonymous with "安" (an; peace and safety); if with a pine, it implies longevity since both pine and chrysanthemum mean living long; and if a cricket (*guoguo*; 蝈蝈) is painted upon chrysanthemum, it implies maintaining one's official title forever since " 蝈 " is homonymous with "官" (*guan*; official).

The tradition of drinking chrysanthemum wine has

Traditional Chinese Painting "Quails and Chrysanthemums"

been kept well in China. It was a must on the Double Ninth Festival, and a kind of auspicious wine for praying for blessings and escaping disasters. The making of chrysanthemum wine was prevailing in the Han and Wei Dynasties. *The Antidotes of the West Capital* (today's Xi'an City) recorded the recipe of making the chrysanthemum wine: on the Double Ninth day, mix the chrysanthemums and the tender chrysanthemum leaves with rice, seal them tightly into the jar, and wait until the next Double Ninth day. Open the jar and the fragrant chrysanthemum wine is brewed. The ancient Chinese people, inspired by the fine wine, would write poems one after another. Tao Yuanming, the Jin Dynasty poet, wrote in his poems that the chrysanthemum wine could get rid of diseases and prevent people from aging. This is the origin of drinking chrysanthemum wine. *The Folk Customs of the Ancient Chu Territory* claimed that wearing Zhuyu, having the Double Ninth Cake, and drinking chrysanthemum wine could lead to longevity. Until the Ming and Qing Dynasties, varieties of herbal medicines were added to the wine for better health care effects.

3.3 Kite-Flying

There's another major custom, kite-flying, on the Double Ninth Festival besides the above-mentioned ascending the height, drinking the chrysanthemum wine, and having the Double Ninth Cake. It was said kite-flying originated from the tale of Huan Jing and Fei Zhangfang, too. It was led by the pigeon that Huan found Fei, the immortal with magic power. In order to memorize the pigeon, people made a paper pigeon and painted by sticking paper onto the bamboo framework. Then they took it to the mountain and flied it. This is the origin of kite-flying.

The Chinese people called kite "纸鹞" (*zhiyao*; paper harrier) at the very beginning. It did not get the name kite until the Five Dynasties (907 A.D. to 960 A.D.). It was controversial about when kite was invented and who invented it. Here're the several popular answers:

The first one was that kite originated from the pre-Qin Era and was invented by Mozi, the great thinker, scientist, educator, militarist, and social activist of ancient China. It was said that Mozi, after three years' experiment, succeeded in making a wooden bird on the Lushan Mountain but it went broken in one day. This wooden bird is the earliest kite in both China and the world at large (about 300 B.C.). That was about more than 2400 years ago. Later, Mozi passed on this craft to his disciple, Lu Ban, who made kite by using bamboo by following the former's desire and design according to *Mozi: The Lu King's Inquiry*. Lu Ban split bamboo into slices, polished them, scorched them on fire supple, and made them into the framework of a magpie which could fly in the sky for three days and nights. The Lushan Mountain is located in today's Weifang, Shandong Province, today's capital of Yuandu, i.e., home to kite. Weifang, famous for its long history and

Sculpture of Lu Ban, West of the Weifang Kite Museum

exquisite craft of kite-making, exported 70% kites of the world. In May of 2006, Weifang Kite was included on the first batch of national intangible heritage list. The headquarters of the International Kite Association is set in this city, too. Nowadays, Weifang has become the center for the world kite cultural communication and is crowned as home to kite by the world people. Like many other folk arts, Weifang kite originates from people's daily recreational activities, and carries people's longing and inspiration.

Tourist tips

The Weifang International Kite Festival

The Weifang International Kite Festival is held in Weifang annually from April 20 to 25. More than 30 countries and regions in the world take part in this festival. It's one of the earliest local festivals in China recognized internationally. Since 1984, more than 33 sessions were successfully held. The model of promoting economy and trade via festivals has been widely used for reference in China. In May of 1983, the Weifang Crafts and Arts Group was invited for attending China Export Commodity Fair, on which, 28 kites of the former drew great attention from the participants at home and abroad, esp. the 50 meter long kite with a dragon head and a centipede body, which stunned the audience. At the fair, David Cheknev, the Chairman of the Seattle Kite Association of the United States, was greatly impressed with Weifang kites and brought some of them back to the U. S. It was this coincidence that pushed Weifang kites to the international stage.

According to statistics, during the International Kite Festival, there were nearly 600 thousand people who came to Weifang for sports game, theatrical performances, economic and trade negotiations, sightseeing, international exchanges, news report, and cultural exchanges, etc.

Address: Weifang is located in the Shandong Peninsula, about 213.3 km away from Jinan City, the capital city of Shandong Province. Trains and buses are available.

Time: from April 20 to 25 annually

The second saying is that kite was invented by Han Xin, the great militarist and strategist at the beginning of the Han Dynasty. *The Night Kite Stories* written by Zhao Xin of the Tang

Dynasty recorded that Xiang Yu and Liu Bang (the former is the founder of the Western Dynasty while the latter the rival of the former, claiming to be the West Chu Kingdom Supreme Ruler, at the end of the Qin Dynasty) had originally reached an agreement that the territory between Chu and Han was marked by the Honggou River (today's Jialu River, in Nanrong County, Henan Province); however, the latter followed the advice of Zhang Liang and Chen Ping (both are Liu Bang's counselors) and decided to annihilate the former's troops by capitalizing on their difficulties. So Liu Bang and Han Xin (a

Children Flying Kites

097

resourceful counselor and a general of Liu Bang) chased after Xiang's troops and surrounded them. Actually there was only a small fraction of soldiers who followed Xiang and the food was in great shortage. Liu wanted to trick his rivals into collapse instead of by hard fighting. At this moment, Han gave birth to a scheme. He designed the framework of a kite and completed it with a carpenter with the surname Wu from Nantong within the Chu territory. Wu tied three bamboo whistles of different sizes to the frame of the kite. After the successful trial flying of the kite, Han summoned the soldiers who were adept at crafts to join in kite-making. And the military camp became into a kite workshop. With the joint efforts, many kites were made, with nutshell or gourd whistles tied.

When the night fell, the kites were flied to the sky, whistles blowing with melancholy melodies, in the meanwhile, the Han soldiers sang the Chu folk songs accompanied by the whistles. The Chu soldiers, haunted with the melody of their hometown, were deeply homesick and disintegrating soon.

In the wake of the Tang Dynasty, flying-kite for military use was converted to recreational activity of young people and children. In the Song Dynasty, kite-flying had become a popular celebration for recreational or joyous occasion. Flying-kite had become a kind of feat, too. People would fly kites on the following occasions: the temple fair, market, festivals, or games. At the end of the Southern Song Dynasty, the craftsman of making kites had appeared.

Family Flying Kite

Kite-flying is popular in China, esp. in south China. Around the Double Ninth Festival, since the southern part of China enjoys cooler climate and stronger monsoon, it's suitable for people to fly kites when they ascend the height or have an autumn hiking with their family members.

Kite-flying is endowed with many implications, mainly represented in two aspects: one is to "ushering in good luck"; another is "sending off bad luck".

Let's look at "ushering in good luck" first. Kite-flying is endowed with praying for blessings and goodwill. In some places, villagers will hold solemn ceremonies, such as laying an incense burner on the table and praying for pleasant weathers and bump harvests.

The traditional kites are usually painted with auspicious patterns or pictures. In the past thousands of years, our ancestors not only created beautiful characters and paintings by using their intellect and wisdom but also the auspicious patterns which demonstrated their aspirations for beautiful life. These characters, pictures and patterns, symbolizing happiness, good luck, and goodwill, catering to people's aesthetic taste, with China's traditions and folk customs infused, are greatly applauded by people.

There're a lot of patterns for good luck; for example, in the south of China, kites with bats(*bianfu*; 蝙蝠) are popular. "蝙蝠" is homonymous with "遍富" (*bianfu*; great wealth) and 遍 福 (*bianfu*; great blessing), and thus being the symbol of blessing. The other patterns for blessing include "鱼" (*yu*; fish, meaning plenty of)and "如意"(*ruyi*, literally meaning "as one wishes", an S-shaped ornament object, usu. made of jade, as a symbol of good luck).

Apart from the above-mentioned ones, dragon, phoenix, and qilin (or kirin) are auspicious creatures in Chinese people's mind. Dragon is the symbol of Chinese people and an idol for worshipping in China. That's why Chinese people call them the descendants of dragon; phoenix is crowned as the king of birds; and *qilin* is a kind of sacred creature in ancient Chinese mythology, a symbol for good luck.

On the contrary, "sending off bad luck" goes like the following: people wrote their names on the kites, flied them to the sky, cut the string, and let it go freely. In this way, people thought "bad air would be sent off", and disasters would be driven off. From the very beginning, flying-kite was closely linked to religious activities of primitive people, who could not prevent themselves from being struck by diseases and natural disasters and did not know what caused pain and poverty, either, had to resort to deities and spirits for blessings owing to the fact that they lived in an age with extremely backward development of science and technology and low productivity.

Therefore, no matter how beautiful the kites are, people must cut the string to send off the bad air; in the meanwhile, the kites which dropped on the ground could not be flied again to avoid catching the bad air. This kind of custom is called flying free kite among the folks.

The custom of sending off the bad air also exists in other countries; for example, the North Korean people will write their sufferings on the paper slips and tie them to the kites. They will cut the string when the kites fly up to the sky, thinking "the bad air" has gone.

In Chaozhou and Shantou, Guangdong Province, quite a lot of superstitious people believe that the Double Ninth day can bring about a change of luck. So they will fly kites, which means letting go the bad luck and embracing the good luck. People attempt to fly their kites higher for sending off the bad luck. Nevertheless, many kites' string is broken before they are flied to the sky. That is why there's an old saying in this region,

"On the Double Ninth day, the kites with broken string are everywhere." It's a taboo to pick the wild kites which drop on the ground.

In Fuzhou City, Fujian Province, it's controversial whether picking the others' kites will catch the bad luck. But Fuzhou people believe that it's an omen if the kite's string is broken before it flies to the sky on the Double Ninth Festival. It is even not allowed to mention broken kite string, which will induce disasters. In this region, broken string is a metaphor for the following tragedy: a woman's husband dies or the marriage is denied before she's married or only after she's married. The local people are really sick of broken kite string.

In Huizhou, Guangdong Province, kite-flying is a major custom of spending the Double Ninth Festival. This custom was not only spread among the folks, but also recorded in *The Annals of Huizhou Prefecture* during the reign of the Guangxu Emperor (1875 A.D.—1908 A.D.) of the Qing Dynasty. The local kite, different from its original shape, is generally square, with a tail. It looks like the God of Door, stuck on the door of every household for protecting the whole family, a possible simplification of deity-like kite. It's an easy job to make a kite in this region. People bind two bamboo slices, one being vertical and another being horizontal, stick a piece of square paper onto the frame, and tie a tail to it. Then the kite is ready for flying. There's another kind of kite, bigger, but with no tail, called Grandma Kite, which can fly stably and steadily in the sky.

Sweeping tombs of ancestors

The Double Ninth Festival, along with the New Year's Eve, the Tomb Sweeping Festival, and the Ghost Festival, is one of the four festivals to pay homage to ancestors. Here's the origin of the custom of sweeping tombs and offering sacrifices to ancestors of the Double Ninth Festival: it was customary for people to ascend the height for escaping disasters. Even nowadays, in Tonglu of Zhejiang Province, Puxian of Fujian Province, Taiwan, and Singapore, people sacrifice pork and mutton to ancestors, which is the so-called autumn sacrifice. The descendants of Confucius, living in the Pearl River Delta of Guangdong, worship their ancestors at the Fengming Tomb, located in Baiyun District of Guangzhou City every Double Ninth Festival. In Puxian of Fujian, the local people will sweep their ancestors' tombs and worship their ancestors while ascending the height. In this region, there's a saying which goes as "The Tomb-Sweeping Day in Spring is not as significant as that in Autumn" since more people will go for worshipping their ancestors on the Double Ninth Festival than on the Tomb-Sweeping Festival in March. In the meanwhile, Sept. 9th is also the day when Mazu , the Goddess of Sea, flied to heaven and became an immortal. The local people go to the Mazu Temple in Meizhou or the Temple of Mazu's Ancestors in Gangli Village for praying for blessings. All in all, there're two festivals for worshipping ancestors in this region: spring and autumn worship. The custom of sweeping tombs is well-kept in the suburb of Fuzhou City or in its suburban counties on the Double Ninth Festival.

Sweeping tombs on the Double Ninth day conforms to the reality of the mountainous area since it's inconvenient for people to go for sweeping tombs which are generally located in the mountains and covered by luxuriant grass or trees on the Tomb Sweeping Festival when it rains very often. People always have difficulties in paving their way in the wildness on wet, rainy days. But it's totally different on the Double Ninth Festival when it's cool and dry, and suitable for people's going out for sweeping tombs while appreciating the autumn sceneries by ascending the height. Furthermore, since the Double Ninth Festival is very close to the National Day holiday, it's convenient for those people who work in other places to ask for leave and join in their families for sweeping tombs. People will bring plenty of sacrifices, incense, and candles for worshipping their ancestors on the basis of one or more families. Many people in Hong Kong will have an autumn tour after paying homage to their ancestors. So there's always traffic jam on the roads to cemeteries.

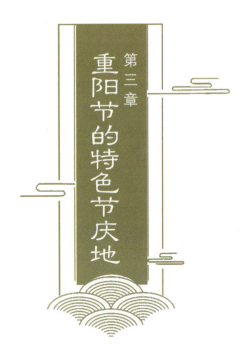

第三章

重阳节的特色节庆地

　　重阳节在我国有着悠久的历史，流传至今，已经成为老百姓生活中一直践行的节庆活动。1989 年，我国把重阳节定为"老人节"，取九月九日"久久"长寿之意。2006 年国务院又将"重阳节"确定为我国"非物质文化遗产"。时至今日，重阳节是杂糅了多种民俗为一体而形成的传统节日。庆祝重阳节习俗普遍为出游赏景、登高远眺、观赏菊花、遍插茱萸、吃重阳糕、饮菊花酒等活动。然而，即便是有着同样的节日习俗，在不同地区自然环境和地域文化的影响下，也会形成当地独具特色的节庆风格。事实上，正是因为这些独具特色的节庆文化丰富了我国重阳节的节日内涵，使得节日更加丰富多彩。

　　重阳节最重要的节日活动之一就是登高，故重阳节又叫登高节。农历九月九日，秋高气爽，登高远望，啸咏骋怀，活动筋骨，所以，人们于重阳登高，在时令上是最合适不过的。从历史源流来看，这与古人的山岳崇拜息息相关。在中国古书《礼记》中就写到"在山林川谷和丘陵地区，烟雾缭绕、有风有雨，是神居住之地。"古代先民生存环境极其艰苦，大多依靠采集和狩猎谋生。大山中生长的各种植物、栖息的飞禽走兽以及潺潺溪流，使人类得以生存繁衍。如果逢高温干旱，山间密林可避高温炙烤；洪水袭来，攀上高山可躲灭顶之灾。此外，古人认为山上云雾缭绕，为呼风雨唤雷电之神龙所居。而且，高山的雷电可以带来火种，利用火可以吃到化腥膻的熟食。因此，古人对山既敬畏又充满崇拜，"登山祈福"的习俗早在春秋战国时期已流行开来。持此观点的人还将"崇"字本身作为旁证：崇，由"山""宗"组成，蕴含有尊崇、敬畏之意。登高"辞青"的说法则源于大自然中的节气。重阳为秋节，节后天气渐凉，草木开始凋零，重阳节登山"辞青"与古人在阳春三月春游"踏青"相对应。

　　在众多的登高活动中又以泰山登高最为出名。泰山位于山东省泰安市中部，素有"五岳之首"之称。传说泰山为盘古开天辟地后其头颅幻化而成，因此中国人自古崇拜泰山，有"泰山安，四海皆安"的说法。历代帝王君主多在泰山进行封禅和祭祀，各朝文人雅士亦喜好来此游历，并留下许多诗文佳作。在古人看来，东方是生命之源，希望和吉祥的象征。而古代汉族先民又往往把雄伟奇特的东岳视为神灵，把山神作为祈求风调雨顺的对象来崇拜。于是，地处东方的泰山便成了"万物孕育之所"的"吉祥之山"、"神灵之宅"。受"天命"而称帝的"天子"更把泰山看成是国家统一，权力的象征。为答谢天帝的"授命"之恩，也必到泰山封禅祭祀。自秦汉至明清，历代皇帝到泰山封禅 27 次。历代帝王借助泰山的神威巩固自己的统治，使泰山的神圣地位被抬到了无以复加的程度。因此重阳节这天，只要在条件允许的情况下，当地人和来自五湖四海的人都前往泰山游玩，观光我国大好河山的同时，祈求来年吉祥平安，健康顺利。

如今，泰山每年 9 月都要举办国际登山节。这时秋高气爽，风景秀丽，交通方便，更使之成为国内近年来具有较高知名度的一个

○泰山——五岳独尊

大型旅游节日。从 1987 年 9 月举办第一届泰山国际登山节以来，至今已经成功举办了 30 届，来自世界各国及国内的来宾和登山健儿欢聚一堂，参加各种节日活动，如徒步登山比赛、自行车登山比赛。

泰山国际登山节期间，还举办泰山优秀历史文化歌舞表演、"泰安摄影艺术展""泰山石文化展""泰山文物珍宝展""泰山盆景展""泰山画展"等丰富多彩的文化艺术活动。登山节除每年评选出登山状元外，还大力组织经贸交易活动，每年都有几十个参展团，推出多种名优产品参加展销；

○泰山

○泰山国际登山节

108

还举办科技、人才交流会，交流最新科技成果、收集科技人才信息，集海内外人文风光旅游、体育比赛、经贸洽谈、科技交流、艺术展览于一身，每年吸引成千上万名海内外游客来此观光旅游。

旅游小贴士

泰　　山

泰山又名岱山、东岳、泰岳，位于山东省中部。主峰玉皇顶海拔 1545 米，气势雄伟磅礴，有"五岳之首""天下第一山"之称。泰山被古人视为"直通帝座"的天堂，成为百姓崇拜、帝王告祭的神山。

泰山风景名胜区是世界自然与文化双重遗产、世界地质公园、国家 AAAAA 级旅游景区、国家级风景名胜区、全国重点文物保护单位。

泰山风景以壮丽著称。重叠的山势，厚重的形体，苍松巨石的烘托，云烟的变化，使它在雄浑中兼有明丽，静穆中透着神奇。自然的泰山，彰显着自然的神奇；文化的泰山，印证着文化的神圣。

泰山是中华民族的象征，是灿烂东方文化的缩影，是"天人合一"思想的寄托之地，是中华民族精神的家园。

饮食：煎饼、烧烤、赤鳞鱼、豆腐宴、野菜宴、枣糕、药膳宴。

特产：石敢当、板栗、肥城桃、宁阳大枣、墨玉、泰山灵芝。

二、
江西秋社节

在我国广阔的疆域里，重阳节期间除了有登高赏菊等传统活动之外，它对于我国的江西来说也是一个谷物收获的季节。江西自古以来物产富饶、人文荟萃，素有"物华天宝、人杰地灵"之誉。江西是我国主要稻产区，气候温暖，日照充足，雨量充沛，每年可以种植水稻两或 3 茬，农历九月大致在公历 9 至 10 月之间，正是江西主要稻产区的秋收时节。赶在秋天即将过去的时候收割晚稻是江西省重阳节的一大农业生活特色。江西过重阳在晚上，白天是一整天的收割、打场。晚上月上树梢，人们享用美味菜肴，待吃过晚饭后，人们三三两两地走出家门，爬上附近山头，点上火光，谈天说地，等到鸡叫才回家。夜里登山，许多人都摘几把野菊花，回家插在女儿的头上，用以避邪。江西省德兴市等地人们于每年 9 至 10 月间晚稻收获完毕后，在农家设办祭品以祭祀神灵，名曰秋社，一以报土谷，一以庆丰年。

秋社节又称赶秋节、交秋节，南方很多少数民族都有这个节日，它是在秋收前或立秋前举行的以娱乐、互市、男女青年交往与庆祝丰收即将到来等为内容的大型民间节日活动。在湘西花垣县以及周边苗族地区，每年立秋日苗族同胞都要举行热闹的赶秋节。赶秋节这天，当地群众停下手中的农活，穿上节日的盛装，结伴成群，从四面八方的村寨来到赶秋的集上，欢聚在山坡上，观看吹笙、演戏、武术、舞狮子、耍龙灯、上刀梯等娱乐节目，并且亲自参与打秋千、打球等娱乐活动，同时还进行物资交流。青年们则多利用这次一年一遇的机会物色对象、谈情说爱。活动完毕时，由众人选出两位有声望的人装扮成"秋老人"，向大家预祝丰收和幸福。

○ 苗族赶秋节

江西重阳节要办酒席，大吃大喝后，到山上登高，购买柑橘从山上往下扔，如果扔到了拣橘子的人身上，霉运就转移到了别人身上。节日期间当地的特色饮食主要是五色糕，办宴席时的最大的特点就是"五味五色"，其中五色是指"红、白、黑、绿、黄"，五味是指"酸、甜、苦、辣、咸"。在当地，还有重阳节抛掷某物以转运的习俗。

重阳节是最好的赏秋时期，中国南方还有些山区村落保留了"晒秋"特色。去乡村赏民俗、看晒秋，已成为乡村旅游的一种时尚，尤其是江西婺源的山村"晒秋"近年来声名鹊起。"晒秋"是一种典型的农俗现象，具有极强的地域特色。生活在湖南、江西、安徽等地山区的村民，由于当地地势复杂，村庄平地极少，只好利用房前屋后及自家窗台屋顶架晒、挂晒农作物，久而久之就演变成一种传统农俗现象。这种村民晾晒农作物的特殊生活方式和场景，逐步成了画家、摄影家追逐、创作的素材，并塑造出诗意般的"晒秋"称呼。发展至今，不少地方的这种晒秋习俗慢慢淡化，然而在江西婺源的篁岭古村，晒秋已经成了农家喜庆丰收的"盛典"。随着果蔬的成熟，篁岭每年九月九日也开始进入晒秋旺季，并举办隆重的晒秋节。篁岭晒秋被文化部评为"最美中国符号"之后，其更演变成提升乡村旅游的"图腾"和名片，每年吸引数十万人去婺源赏秋拍摄。

○江西婺源晒秋

三、
开封菊花会

　　菊花，又叫黄花，属菊科，品种繁多。我国是菊花的故乡，自古培种菊花就很普遍。菊是长寿之花，又为文人们赞美作凌赏菊霜不屈的象征，所以人们爱它、赞它，故常举办大型的菊展。菊展自然多在重阳举行，重阳又称菊花节，而菊花又称九花。赏菊也就成了重阳节习俗的组成部分。宋代《东京楚华录》中记载：每到九月重阳的时候，人们都外出赏菊，菊花也有很多的种类，其中花蕊是黄白的，称为"万龄菊"；花蕊是粉红色的，称为"桃花菊"；白色花蕊的称为"木香菊"；形状是圆的黄色菊花，称为"金龄菊"；纯白的大菊花，称为"喜容菊"，总之菊花种类繁多、五花八门。明代，在《陶庵梦忆》中记载：兖州绍绅家每到赏菊之日，桌子、炕、灯、炉子等都是用菊花图样制作而成，栩栩如生。清代《燕京岁时记》中记载了当时重阳赏菊的盛况：菊花在当时又被称为"九花"，每到重阳的时候，富贵人家，用数百盆菊花摆满房前屋后，远远望去，就像小山一样，因此得名"九花山子"，四面堆积的菊花称为"九花塔"。至今，重阳节期间，各大公园也仍组织大型菊展，并将菊缚扎成各类动植物、人物等造型，十分美观。在我国重阳节期间开办菊展最为有名的是河南开封和上海两地，各处不同的地域，同样的民俗活动下体现着不一样的人文景观。

○河南开封菊花展

菊花是开封市"市花"，开封菊花栽培历史悠久，菊花的数量、品种、栽培技术不断增加和提高。开封菊花，不但花朵肥大、色泽纯正，而且高矮适度。菊花品种1200多个。开封菊花会始办于1983年。开封也是唯一一座以菊花为主题每年举行一次年会的城市。一年一度秋风劲，岁岁黄花分外香。开封菊花会就像一颗大树，深深植根于开封人民心中。菊花会所产生的影响，就其广度而言，已远远超过了开封的地界，名扬海内外；就其深度而言，已远远超出了"赏菊"的特定含义。菊花会作为一种成功的载体和平台，展示着开封深厚的文化底蕴，演绎着经贸、旅游的大戏，推动着开封的精神文明建设和物质文明建设。

开封菊花会植根于古城，有其深远的历史渊源。菊花会远在唐代就初具规模。唐代诗人刘禹锡对开封菊花也进行了描述。北宋时，开封菊花更是闻名遐迩。每逢重阳节，不仅民间有花市赛花，而且宫廷内也养菊、插菊花枝、挂菊花灯、饮菊花酒，甚至还开菊花会。《东京梦华录》中也有游人赏菊的相关记载。明清时期，开封养菊、赏菊之风依然盛行，清代乾隆皇帝南巡来到开封禹王台赏菊时，就留下了"枫叶梧青落，霜花菊白堆"的著名诗句，这诗句被刻在当今禹王台公园保存的乾隆御碑上。中华人民共和国成立后，特别是改革开放以来，随着人民群众物质文化生活水平不断提高，开封人民酷爱菊花的情结更加浓厚，每年重阳期间，花市售卖菊花和沿街叫卖菊花成为一道独特的风景。号称是菊花、茱萸故乡的西峡县，在隋唐时，就因当地重阳节俗兴盛，菊花山声名远播，而专设"菊潭县"，前后长达 250 年。据史料记载，唐代大诗人李白、孟浩然、杜甫、贾岛、白居易、李商隐都曾到西峡菊花山登高赏菊，宋朝的苏辙、元初大诗人元好问都游览过菊花山，并留下了丰富的诗篇。

○ 上海菊花展

除了北方的开封，在南方同样有一个城市每年重阳节也会举办菊花展以此庆祝节日，这座城市就是上海。上海每年在重阳节期间于豫园开办金秋菊花会，菊花会秉承着中国几千年悠久的人文历史。

在有着数百年历史、凝聚了中国传统文化精髓、积淀了深厚人文底蕴的豫园，举办传统花会，是政通人和、国泰民安的标志。金秋菊花会以新巧、高贵、珍异三项评分定高下。菊花会以龙为主题，整个展场布局为双龙缠绕，呈环抱之势。借鉴中国古典诗词的艺术结构，顺应豫园原有的空间关系，以起、承、转、合形成发展序列，层层递进，逐步展开。同时切合《易经》乾卦的五个卦象，象征事物发展的五个阶段，隐喻中华民族发展的不同阶段历史。菊花会菊花品种多：上海菊花会共展出菊花1000多种，奇花、新品、珍品汇聚一堂，同时展出"帅旗""绿牡丹""墨菊""十丈珠帘""绿衣红裳"等中国五大菊花珍品。菊花会布展规模大：菊花会总布展面积达9万平方米，37个大型立体景点，各省市展台126个，并设室内精品、造型菊、大立菊、悬崖菊、十八花道、百菊赛、塔菊共七大展区。菊花展展览时间长：上海地区属于亚热带湿润季风气候，展出期间，上海地区的天气恰逢晴朗时节，每天都有大量市民前往赏花，所以，组委会每年都会适当延长展期。

旅游小贴士

开　封

开封是河南省地级市，简称汴，古称东京、汴京，为八朝古都。位于黄河中下游平原东部，地处河南省中东部，东与商丘相连，西与郑州毗邻，南接许昌和周口，北与新乡隔黄河相望。开封是中原经济区的核心城市之一，河南省中原城市群和沿黄"三点一线"黄金旅游线路三大中心城市之一。开封已有两千七百多年的历史，是首批中国历史文化名城之一，中国八大古都之一。北宋时开封更是当时世界第一大城市。开封是世界上唯一一座城市中轴线从未变动的都城，城摞城遗址在世界考古史和都城史上少有。开封亦是《清明上河图》的原创地，有"东京梦华"之美誉。

开封有众多的文物古迹、包括国家级文物保护单位13处，省级38处，市级26处，县级136处。闻名遐迩的铁塔、相国寺、包公祠、延庆观、繁塔等，具有较高的历史文化价值。作为河南三大石刻集中地之一，开封馆藏和各名胜古迹中保存着上自汉代、下止民国的各类石刻珍品1000余件，是研究历史、科学技术和书法艺术的宝贵资料。

○ 开封古城

四、
铜陵龙烛会

农历九月初九日的重阳佳节，安徽各地有登高、赏菊、喝菊花酒、吃重阳糕、插茱萸等习俗，其中登高望远是重阳节的传统习俗。每年各地老年协会都会组织很多老人去登高望远，这已成为安徽地区老年人在重阳节的必要活动之一。此外，吃重阳糕、插重阳旗、办龙烛会也是当地独具特色的习俗。重阳旗是用一根细篾子做旗杆、用彩色纸做小三角旗，上面有许多小孔，有的还印有文字或花式图案，插在重阳糕上，这样的重阳糕吃法更具特色。

重阳节举办龙烛会，主要在安徽铜陵一带流传。削竹马为戏，据说可以驱逐瘟疫；点上龙烛，以迎山神。蜡烛是古代的主要照明工具之一，而"龙烛"，就是以龙的图案装饰的蜡烛，多用于婚

○龙烛，也叫喜烛，多用于婚庆场合

嫁之时。竹马戏是一种古朴而稀少的民间歌舞小戏，享有"戏曲活化石"之誉，来源于"跑竹马"表演活动。漳州地区曾经流行于漳浦、南靖、华安、平和、龙溪、海澄、东山等县，尤以漳浦县最为盛行。安徽、台湾也有竹马戏，俗称"布马阵"，又称"阵戏"。

"跑竹马"，顾名思义就是骑着竹马表演。竹马是用竹篾扎成马的形状，外蒙绸布（有红、黑、赤、青、花、白等多种颜色），就成了一匹活灵活现的马。演出时，竹马的前部挂在演员前齐腹高处，后部安置在背后腰椎处，看起来演员就像真的骑在马上。"跑竹马"表演的特点重在跑，以跑入场，以跑收场，贯穿始终，即跑中见阵、阵中有情，跑出姿态、跑出阵势。

○江苏邳州的跑竹马表演

竹马戏是戏曲的一个剧种，是从民间歌舞"跑竹马"表演发展而来的地方剧种。竹马戏主要流行于福建沿海与台湾一带，在当地民间歌谣、小调、南曲等说唱技艺的基础上，吸收融合了闽南木偶戏、梨园戏的一些唱腔和表演程式而逐渐形成，已有三百余年历史。

 五、
潮汕菊花宴

重阳又称重九，潮汕重阳节是广东潮汕汉族民俗及民间祭祀的重要节日。这天在潮汕，有各种具有地方特色的汉族民俗活动。因为它的节期就在农历九月初九。古人以九为阳数，故又称之为"重阳"。潮汕汉族民间，直接称它作"九月九"。

在潮汕，至迟到南宋初年，就有重阳登高宴集的风俗。潮阳东山方广洞侧，有一处纪游的摩崖石刻，记载了重阳节的盛况，在这一天，文人墨客或携酒入山寺游玩为乐，小儿咸于高处竞放风筝，文人们赋诗言志，这些诗作，绘出了一幅明代文人重阳节日风俗图。与前代的重阳节日习俗相比，"登高宴饮、簪菊泛萸"等旧俗之外，清代又有"竞放风筝"的新时尚。

重阳节祭祖也是潮汕的一个节日习俗。在古代重阳祭祖的都是家境比较清贫者，他们无力在每个祖先的忌辰都祭拜，便在这一天做个总的祭拜，求得祖宗谅解。潮汕人于此日登临韩山、金山瞻仰韩愈、马发等文宗武魁的墓也为数不少，并写了很多诗作纪念他们。

潮汕重阳节保持着中国传统的风俗，如高人雅士登高游赏，饮酒赋诗，老百姓翻晒衣物书籍、椅柜，颇有古意。在潮安、澄海且有一处结缘风习，即炸油麻丸分送亲友。丸与缘同音（粤语读音），意在结缘。另旧时潮州戏班自初一日起至初九晚上要食斋，称食九皇斋。自初一日起全班人员穿白衫裤，天天焚香敬奉，初九晚上，全体敬拜（连同玄武山佛祖和戏神田元帅一起拜）。民间也有拜九皇者。在泰国潮籍华侨裔食九皇斋则更隆重，自初一至初九或初十，普遍有食九皇斋，祀拜皇神之俗。他们所祭祀的九皇神，与中国神书上所说的北斗辰宿不同，也与潮汕本土汉族民间传说的人皇九个头，有九个兄弟，分管九州的九皇神不同。他们拜的九皇神，传说原是九个贼，后被观音大士收服，改邪为正，大慈大悲，做了许多善事，成为佛门的大弟子，而受人们的崇拜，构成了有异于本土的潮汕华侨民俗的一部分。

古往今来，潮汕人家，世代相沿，"九九"重阳有赏菊、餐菊、饮菊、插菊等风俗。古医籍《神农本草经》中有"菊花，久服利血气、轻身、耐老、延年"之记载。故古人赞美菊花为"延寿客"，其功可知矣。在当地重阳节期间也形成了独具特色的"菊花宴"。菊花宴，毋庸置疑都是用菊花做成的宴会食物，在菊花宴中包含了以下几种菊花制作的食物。

菊花鸡汤——将菊花撕瓣清洗干净，晾干，然后将生鸡肉刀切成薄片；用暖锅盛着预先清炖的鸡肉（骨）汤，原汁原叶，调料用植物油、特等鱼露、少许味精等，当加热汤沸之时，投下鸡肉片滚烫熟后酌量投入—撮菊花瓣于汤中，拌匀即成，入口鸡肉嫩滑爽口，菊瓣美味清香。这道名馔也即时尚的

○菊花鸡汤

清代京城"菊花火锅"，清香可口，惹人馋涎。

菊花肉丝——将菊花清洗干净，晾干、撕成丝，选用瘦猪肉切成肉丝，用豆粉或薯粉加入精盐和水充分拌匀。然后以铁锅置于旺火上，投入花生油旺火炒至肉丝松散发白时，再加点特级鱼露、味精，再投入菊花丝略炒待拌合均匀即成，黄白菊丝，鲜美艳丽，美味清香，嫩滑爽口，令人喜爱。

菊花虾仁——鲜虾仁用刀切一口，剔去肠中内容物（勿剖开成片），用生葱、生姜切成丝适量，将黄白菊花洗净撕丝。铁锅置于炉上旺火加油炒至虾仁肉质变红之时，以鱼露、味精及食醋为调味料，此时速将菊花丝投入，略炒均匀即成，虾仁嫩滑，秋菊香美，海

○菊花肉丝

122

鲜美味，口感殊佳，
食家无不赞美。

菊花鲈鱼——清
秋鲜鲈肥美，肉白如
银。先将鲈鱼刮去鳞，
剖腹除去内脏，洗净
血污，浸渍后沥去水
分，置于盘中，用生葱、

○菊花虾仁

红辣椒、生姜切丝，加酱油、味精调料，并用黄白色菊花撕瓣相间
铺放于鲈鱼身上，隔水旺火蒸 10—15 分钟即熟，色泽鲜艳，菊鱼味
香，入嘴更觉清香爽口。

菊花粥——大米 100 克，洗净，加水煮成粥，当白稀粥将黏稠
之时，将清洗干净的黄白色菊花切碎约 20 克加入稀粥中，拌匀即成。
美食菊花粥具有清肝明目、祛风清热、利气血、轻身耐老延年之功效。

○菊花粥

III

The Special Local Celebrations of The Double Ninth Festival

The Double Ninth Festival has a long history in China and has been observed by ordinary people. In 1989, the Chinese government set it officially as the Seniors' Day by drawing the implication of jiujiu (久久 ; longevity) which is homonymous with the ninth day of the ninth month in the Chinese lunar calendar. In 2006, it was included on the national intangible cultural heritage list by the Chinese government. So far, the Double Ninth Festival has become a traditional holiday which integrates various kinds of folk customs, including touring, ascending the height for looking into the distance, enjoying chrysanthemum flowers, wearing *zhuyu*, having the Double Ninth Cake, and drinking chrysanthemum wine, etc. Nevertheless, even the same festival traditions will be observed in different ways in different places with different natural surroundings and local culture. As a matter of fact, it is these special festival celebrations that enrich the contents of the Double Ninth Festival.

1. Mount Tai International Mountaineering Festival

One of the major activities for the Double Ninth Festival is Ascending the Height, and hence its additional name, Height Ascending Festival. The festival falls on the autumn season when it's fine and cool, being suitable for people to climb mountains and build their bodies. In terms of its history, this custom is closely related to the ancient people's worship for mountains. According to the classical Chinese literature, the *Book of Rites*, the ancient people, living in harsh environment, fed on hunting animals and gathering fruits and seeds of plants. Their subsistence mainly relied on plants, birds, animals, and brooks in the mountains. When it was hot and dry, people would hide themselves in the mountain forest from being scorched by the sun; when flooding struck, people climbed onto the mountains from being drown. What's more, the high mountains were covered in thick mists and clouds, which made the ancient people believe that the magic dragon lived there with the power of generating wind, rain, thunder and flash. Additionally, thunder and flash on the top of the mountain would produce fire used for cooking. Thus, the ancient people had great awe and worship for mountains. Actually, the tradition of climbing mountains for blessing had been spread in the Spring and Autumn and the Warring States periods. Here's the evidence: the Chinese character "崇" (chong), composed of "山" (mountain) and "宗" (showing respect for), literally means worshipping the mountain. Another saying related

125

to Ascending to the Height is to say goodbye to the green summer, a counterpart of Spring Hiking in the third month of the Chinese lunar calendar since the Double Ninth Festival is in the autumn season after which the plants will wither day by day.

The most famous activity of Ascending the Height is Mount Tai mountaineering. Mount Tai is located in the middle of Tai'an City of Shandong Province, crowned as the first among the Five Famous Mountains in China. The legend goes that after Pangu, a hero in the ancient Chinese mythology, separated the heaven from the earth, his head was converted to Mount Tai, thus there had been the old saying "A safe and sound Mount Tai, a safe and sound China" since the ancient times. The emperors and monarchs in Chinese history went to Mount Tai for offering sacrifices to heaven and earth while men of letters toured there and left a lot of household poems. In the mind of the ancient people, the east was the origin of life and the symbol of hope and good luck. What's more, the Han ancestors deemed the East Mountain, Mount Tai, being grand and majestic, as deity, which was worshipped for praying for pleasant weather and harvest. Accordingly, Mount Tai became an auspicious mountain, where creatures were given birth to, and the residence of deities. The ancient emperors and monarchs thought they were the sons of heaven: tianzi (天子 , consisting of 天 tian and 子 zi, the former meaning heaven and the latter meaning son), and authorized by heaven for ruling the earth. Consequently, they regarded Mount Tai as the symbol of national unity and power. To express their gratitude to the emperor of heaven, they would go to Mount Tai for offering sacrifices. From the Qin and Han Dynasties to the Ming and Qing Dynasties, the emperors and monarchs resorted to the mysterious power of Mount Tai for consolidating their sovereign, which lifted its sacred position to the greatest extent. That's why people at home and abroad will gather here for praying for peace, prosperity, and health while feasting on the beautiful sceneries on the Double Ninth Festival.

Currently, the International Mount Tai Mountaineering Festival is held every mid-September. It has become one of the privileged festivals in China featuring pleasant weather, beautiful sceneries, and convenient transportation. Since the first session in Sept. of 1987, so far thirty ones has been held, which attracted tourists and mountaineers at home and abroad to take part in various kinds of games, such as mountaineering by hiking, mountaineering by biking, etc.

During the International Mount Tai Mountaineering Festival, varieties of cultural and art activities are held, too, such as the Theatrical Performances on the History and Culture of Mount Tai, Tai'an Photography Art Exhibition, Mount Tai Rock Culture Exhibition, Mount Tai Cultural Treasure Exhibition, Mount Tai Bonsai Exhibition, Mount Tai Painting Exhibition, etc. In the meanwhile, economic and trade activities are promoted rigorously. There're scores of groups of people who exhibit their knockout products annually. What's more, the Scientific and Technological Talent Fair is held annually, featuring exchanges on the latest developments of science and technology and on the talents of science and technology. In short, the above activities, integrating cultural and natural touring, sports games, economic and trade negotiations, scientific and technological communication, and art exhibitions, attract hundreds of thousands of tourists at home and abroad annually.

Tourist tips

Mount Tai

Mount Tai, located in the middle of Shandong Province, has acquired several other names, the Dai Mount, the East Mount, or the Taiyue Mount. Its summit, the Jade Emperor Summit, is 1545 meters above the sea level. Mount Tai, well-known for its grandeur and majesty, is crowned as the First Mountain of China, the First among the Five Famous Mountains. Taken as the paradise leading to the emperor's throne, Mount Tai has become a sacred mountain which people worship and emperors and monarchs offer sacrifices to heaven and earth.

Mount Tai Scenic Spot: It falls on the categories of both world natural and cultural heritages by UNESCO. It is a world geological park and a country-level AAAAA scenic spot under the national protection.

Mount Tai Scenic Spot is well-known for its grandeur and beauty. The capricious rocks and peaks, the luxuriant pines, the mists and clouds endow it with unique beauty and grandeur. The natural Mount Tai is a masterpiece of nature while the cultural Mount Tai demonstrates the charm of culture.

Mount Tai is a symbol of the Chinese nation, a microscope of the glamorous oriental culture, an incarnation of the ancient Chinese philosophy—unity of human and nature, as well as the representation of Chinese people's spirit and soul.

Special local foods: pancake, barbecue, stewed cabbage with tofu , red-scaled fish, tofu banquet, wild vegetable banquet, jujube cake, herbal medicine banquet

Local specialties: Shi Gan Dang (stone inscriptions in Mount Tai with the Chinese characters "石敢当" , regarded as devices of scaring off evil spirits and escaping disasters), chestnuts, Feicheng peach, Ningyang jujube, black jade, ganoderma

2. The Autumn Sacrifice Festival of Jiangxi Province

The Double Ninth Festival, for people in Jiangxi Province, is one for celebrating harvest, apart from ascending the height and enjoying chrysanthemums. Jiangxi Province boasts its rich natural resources and numerous talents. It's one of the major rice-producing areas in China with warm climate, ample sunshine and rain. Two-cropped or three-cropped rice grows here.

According to the Chinese lunar calendar, the ninth month crosses September and October when rice is ripe. Farmers will harvest late rice before the autumn is over. People in Jiangxi Province spend the Double Ninth Festival in the evening since they're busy with reaping rice at daytime. Only when the night falls, people can have time for dinner, after which, they will climb to the top of the nearby mountain with torches, chatting and playing. They won't go back home until roosters crow in the next dawn. Many will pick a bunch of wild chrysanthemums in the mountain and wear them on their daughter's head for driving off the evil spirits. The people in Dexing and some other places, Jiangxi Province, usually offer sacrifices to deities at home after reaping late rice. This is the origin of the Autumn Sacrifice for worshipping the God of Land and the God of Grains as well as celebrating the harvest.

The Autumn Sacrifice Festival, or the Chasing Autumn Festival, or the Autumn Festival, is observed by many ethnic minorities. It's a grand folk activity featuring recreation, marketing, and socializing of young people, and celebrating harvest. In Huayuan County, a Miao autonomous region west of Hunan Province, and in its surrounding Miao ethnic group inhabitations, the Miao people will dress themselves in festive

Girls Dressed in Miao Costumes on the Chasing Autumn Festival

costumes and flock to the market for spending the Chasing
Autumn Festival on the day of Liqiu (beginning of the autumn,
one of the 24 solar terms based on the Chinese lunar calendar).
They gather at the autumn slope watching pipe blowing, drama
performances, martial arts, lion dance, dragon lantern dance,
and stepping on knife ladder, etc., or swing and play ball games
themselves, or trading things while the young people make
full use of this precious opportunity for socializing. Before the
activity is over, two Autumn Elders will be chosen and dressed
up, usually on the basis of reputation, wish people a bump
harvest and happiness next year.

In Jiangxi Province, people will host grand banquets before
climbing onto the mountain, where they throw down the hill
the oranges prepared in advance. It's said the bad luck will
be transferred to those people who're hit by the oranges. The
oranges can be replaced by some other heavy objects, too. The
festive delicacy is the Five-Colored Cake with five tastes, sour,
sweet, bitter, hot, and salty as well as five colors, red, white,
black, green, and yellow.

The Double Ninth Festival is not only the best time
for touring but also for Sun-Bathing Autumn ("晒秋" Drying
Autumn Harvests in the Sun). It has become a trend to go to
villages for witnessing the folk customs and Drying Autumn
Harvests in the Sun, esp. that of the mountain villages in
Wuyuan County, Jiangxi Province. Drying Autumn Harvests
in the Sun is a typical agricultural custom with strong regional

characteristics. The villagers who live in the deep mountains in Hunan, Jiangxi, and Anhui Provinces have to dry the autumn harvests in front of or behind houses, on the window panes, or on the top of roofs since the rock terrain makes the spacious opening precious or unavailable. The special way of drying the autumn crops has been chased by painters and photographers, and hence the poetic name Sun-Bathing Autumn. So far, this kind of custom has been neutralized with the time passing by in many places, but in one of the ancient villages in Wuyuan County of Jiangxi Province, Huanglin, it has become a grand ceremony of celebrating harvest. Around the Double Ninth Festival, the Sun-Bathing Autumn Festival is held annually in this village, which was prized as the most beautiful logo of China by the Cultural Ministry of China. Since then, it has become a totem and a name card of village tour and annually attracts hundreds of thousands of people there for autumn tour and photographing.

3. The Kaifeng Chrysanthemum Fair

The large-scale chrysanthemum exhibitions are often held in many places around the Double Ninth Festival, which explains why it has got another name, the Chrysanthemum Festival and the flower has got another name, Nine Flower, too. Of course, enjoying chrysanthemums has become an important component of the Double Ninth Festival customs. According to *A Reminiscence of Dongjing in its Prime* (Dongjing, the capital city of the Northern Song and Southern Song Dynasties) written in the Southern Song Dynasty, people would go out for enjoying chrysanthemums. During that time, people fostered great varieties of species: those with yellow and white flowers are "Longevity chrysanthemum"; those with pink flowers are "Peach chrysanthemum"; those with white flowers are "Banks' rose chrysanthemum"; those with circular yellow flowers are "Golden age chrysanthemum"; those with pure big flowers are "Happy countenance chrysanthemum", etc. According to *The Dreams of Tao'an* written by Zhang Dai (who styled himself as Tao'an) in the Ming Dynasty, tables, beds, lanterns, and stoves used by Shaoshen's family in Yanzhou of Shandong Province were all decorated with patterns of chrysanthemum when they enjoyed chrysanthemums. Another book, *Annual Customs and Festivals* in Peking, written in the Qing Dynasty recorded the grand occasion of enjoying chrysanthemums: during that time, chrysanthemum was called Nine Flowers. On the Double Ninth Festival, the wealthy families would lay hundreds of pots of chrysanthemum in front of or behind their houses, resembling towers of flowers if looked from distance, hence the name Nine Flower Mountain or Nine Flower Tower. So far, during the Double Ninth Festival, large-scale chrysanthemum exhibitions are held at parks, where chrysanthemums are made into shapes of animals, plants, and figures. The most famous two chrysanthemum exhibitions nationwide are held in Kaifeng, Henan Province, and in Shanghai. The same folk custom is observed with different cultural connotations.

Chrysanthemum is the municipal flower of Kaifeng City, which is famous for its long history of fostering chrysanthemum and its incomparable advantages in number, species, and fostering techniques of chrysanthemum. Kaifeng chrysanthemums boast their big flowers, pure color, and adequate height. There're more than 1200 varieties of chrysanthemums in this city. The Kaifeng Chrysanthemum Fair, initiated in 1983, is the only one in China held annually and thus deeply-rooted in the mind of Kaifeng people. It has exerted great influence at home and abroad and its value has gone far beyond enjoying chrysanthemums itself. The Fair, serving as a media and platform, has succeeded in demonstrating the profound cultural deposit of Kaifeng and bearing the duty of promoting touring and economic exchanges, and thus pushing forward both material and cultural advancement of Kaifeng.

Thirty-Second Session of Chrysanthemum Fair of Kaifeng

The Kaifeng Chrysanthemum Fair, deeply rooted in this ancient city, enjoys a long history. It came into being in the Tang Dynasty, which can be proved by the poem of the Tang poet, Liu Yuxi. In the North Song Dynasty, the Kaifeng chrysanthemum was extremely famous. On the Double Ninth Festival, apart from the chrysanthemum fair and chrysanthemum race for ordinary people, the court also hosted varieties of activities of enjoying chrysanthemum, such as chrysanthemum exhibition, wearing chrysanthemum, hanging chrysanthemum lanterns, drinking chrysanthemum wine, and even chrysanthemum meeting. *A Reminiscence of Dongjing* in its Prime also recorded the grand scene of people's enjoying chrysanthemums. In the Ming and Qing Dynasties, fostering and enjoying chrysanthemums were still prevailing in Kaifeng. The Emperor Qianlong of the Qing Dynasty had written in his poem, "While maple and Chinese parasol leaves turn scarlet and yellow, chrysanthemums bloom white covered by flower-like frost" when he toured the Yuwang Terrace in Kaifeng. The two lines were inscribed onto the imperial stele granted by the emperor. After the founding of People's Republic of China, esp. since the reforming and opening-up policy has been implemented, with the improvement of people's living, the Kaifeng people are more passionate about chrysanthemum. The annual Double Ninth Festival witnesses the spectacle of Kaifeng: chrysanthemums are sold at the flower fair and by the street vendors. The Xixia County, claiming to be the hometown of chrysanthemum and *zhuyu*, enjoyed great reputation for its grand celebrations on the Double Ninth Festival and for its chrysanthemums in the Sui and Tang Dynasties. Hence, it acquired the name Jutan ("菊潭" meaning a pool of chrysanthemums) County, which existed for 250 years in history. According to records, the great Tang poets, Li Bai, Meng Haoran, Du Fu, Jia Dao, Bai Juyi, and Li Shangyin, had ever been to this county for ascending a height and enjoying chrysanthemums. The great Song poet, Su Shi, and the great Yuan poet, Yuan Haowen had been to this county for touring the Chrysanthemum Mountain and left wealth of poems.

Besides the northern city Kaifeng, there's another southern city which hosts chrysanthemum fair for celebrating the Double Ninth Festival, i.e., Shanghai. The Shanghai Chrysanthemum Exhibition is held annually on the Double Ninth Festival at Yu Garden. The chrysanthemum exhibition carries thousands of years' history of China. Yu Garden, with several hundreds of years' history, demonstrating the essence of traditional Chinese culture and the profound humanistic connotations, is a suitable a place for hosting such a traditional chrysanthemum fair. What a harmonious scene! The chrysanthemums which attend the fair will be judged from the three elements: being novel, being noble, and being precious. The chrysanthemum fair is themed with dragon. The whole exhibition venue was highlighted by two dragons entangled with each other. The layout of the exhibition conforms well to the surroundings of

Yu Garden and the five phenomena of *Qiangua* (one of the eight trigrams in *Bagua*, referring to heaven), which indicates the five development phases of things, a manifestation of the different historical periods of the Chinese nation.

This exhibition has three characteristics. Firstly, great varieties of chrysanthemum: there're more than 5000 varieties of chrysanthemum at this exhibition, many of which are novel and precious ones, including the five Chinese traditional precious species—banner chrysanthemum, green peony chrysanthemum, bead curtain chrysanthemum, and color-changed chrysanthemum. Secondly, large scale of the exhibition: the exhibition area amounts to 90 thousand square meters with 37 gardens and 126 exhibition booths. Seven exhibition districts are set: indoor varieties, molded chrysanthemum, cascade chrysanthemum, eighteen corridors

Ancient City Kaifeng

of chrysanthemum, chrysanthemum race, and towered chrysanthemum. Thirdly, long duration of the exhibition: the organizing committee decided to lengthen the exhibition because the pleasant weather attracted large amount of people for enjoying chrysanthemum although, generally speaking, Shanghai is of subtropical, humid monsoon climate.

Tourist tips

Kaifeng

Kaifeng, a prefectural city of Han Province, shortened into bian (汴), named Dongjing (the East Capital) in the ancient times, is the capital city of eight dynasties in Chinese history. It's located in the east of the middle and lower reaches of the Yellow River, the central part of Henan Province, neighboring Zhengzhou (today's capital city of Henan Province) in the west, Xuchang and Zhoukou City in the south, and Xinxiang City in the north. Kaifeng and Xinxiang are separated from each other by the Yellow River. It's one of the key cities of the central economic zone, one of the central city clusters in Henan Province, as well as one of the three core cities on the golden tourist route "Three Spots and One Line" beside the Yellow River. Kaifeng boasts its history of more than 2700 years and is included to the first batch of cultural and historical heritage cities. It is one of the ancient capital cities in China. During the Northern Song Dynasty, it was the largest metropolis in the world. It's the only capital city whose axis had never changed. So you can enjoy stacked city ruins which are seldom seen elsewhere. Kaifeng, being the prototype of Riverside Scene on the Qingming Festival, a world−famous painting made in the Song Dynasty, enjoys the reputation of "the Capital City of Dreamlike Prosperity".

Kaifeng boasts numerous cultural and historical interests, including

13 key cultural and historical heritages under national protection, 38 ones under provincial protection, 26 under municipal protection, and 136 under county-level protection, among which, the well-known Iron Tower, Baogong Temple, Yanqing Taoist Temple, and Fan Tower are of highly cultural and historical values. As one of the places famous for stone inscriptions, Kaifeng preserves varieties of them from the Han Dynasty to the Republic of China in its museums, or in its cultural and historical interests, which are valuable materials for researching on Chinese history, science and technology, and calligraphy.

4. The Tongling Dragon Candle Fair

Ascending a height, enjoying chrysanthemums, drinking chrysanthemum wine, having Double Ninth Cake, and wearing *zhuyu* are the routine customs in Anhui Province on the Double Ninth Festival, among which, the first one is traditional. In addition, the Elders' Association will organize the elders to ascend a height, one of the routine practices in Anhui Province. Having Double Ninth Cake, sticking Double Ninth miniature flags, having Dragon Candle Fair are special local customs. The Double Ninth flags are miniature triangle ones stuck onto the Double Ninth Cake with pricked holes, or printed with Chinese characters or pictures.

The Dragon Candle Fair prevails in Tongling, Anhui Province. People perform bamboo horse opera for driving away plague and light dragon candle for honoring the God of Mountain. Candles are used for lighting in ancient times and Dragon Candles are those decorated with dragon patterns, mainly applied for wedding ceremony. The Bamboo Horse

Opera is a kind of simple, precious local opera, which enjoys the reputation of "live fossil of opera". It originates from the performance of running bamboo horses. It had ever been popular in Zhangpu, Nanjing, Hua'an, Pinghe, Longxi, Haicheng, and Dongshan counties in Zhangzhou, Fujian Province, esp. in Zhangpu County. There's Bamboo Horse Opera in Taiwan, too, popularly called "Bumazhen (lay a horse array)" or "Zhen Opera".

Running Bamboo Horse literally means performance by riding bamboo horse. Bamboo horse is made by binding thin bamboo slices into the frame of a horse and then covering it by silk cloth, usu. in red, black, blue, white color or being colored. Actors and actresses will stand in the middle opening of the bamboo horse and perform. It seems that they're riding on real horses. Running Bamboo Horses lies in running, beginning with running and ending with running, too. The horse array has been changed with running, too.

Ancient Town Tongling in Anhui Province

Bamboo Horse Opera, a kind of local one evolved from running bamboo horse, mainly prevails in the coastal area of Fujian Province and Taiwan. Based on the local folk songs, tunes, and the Nanqu Opera, it absorbs Puppet Performance of the southern part of Fujian, vocal sounds and formulated performance of other local operas and has formed its own style. So far, it enjoys the history of over 300 years.

5. Chrysanthemum Banquet of Chaozhou and Shantou in Guangdong Province

The Double Ninth Festival is an important holiday for Han people to practice folk customs and offering sacrifices in Chaozhou and Shantou of Guangdong Province. The local Han people calls *jiu yue jiu* (the ninth day of the ninth month in the Chinese lunar calendar).

The latest record about ascending a height and having a banquet in Chaozhou and Shantou was at least at the beginning of the Southern Song Dynasty. Beside Fangguang Cave, the Dongshan Mountain, Chaoyang, Guangdong, there's a cliff stone inscription which describes the grand celebration of the Ming Dynasty people on the Double Ninth Festival when men of letters would ascend a height relaxing, or writing poems, which depicted their ways of festive celebration in the Ming Dynasty while carrying wine whereas children flied kites on the height. Compared with the previous festive customs, the new fashion of flying kites was added to the old ones of ascending a height and drinking as well as wearing yellow chrysanthemum.

Worshipping ancestors is another festive custom of Chaozhou and Shantou. In the ancient times, generally speaking, the poor people would offer sacrifices to their ancestors on the Double Ninth Festival because they could not afford to do so on the other occasions of honoring their ancestors. They hoped for securing the forgiveness of their ancestors by this way. Many people would climb the Hanshan Mountain, or the Jinshan Mountain for worshipping Han Yu, a master in prose writing, or Ma Fa, a national hero in defending against the Yuan invaders (the northern nomadic tribes who became the rulers of the Yuan Dynasty and ruled China from 1206—1368) and wrote poems to commemorate them.

People in Chaozhou and Shantou well kept the Chinese traditional customs of celebrating the Double Ninth Festival: men of letters will ascend a height for touring, and write poems while drinking wine whereas the folks will dry clothes, books, and furniture in the sun. there's a special local custom, that is, jieyuan(结缘) (making friends), distributing youmawang (油麻王) (fried rice cake with sesame) since "缘" is homonymous with "王". Another special local custom is Jiuhuang(九皇 meaning nine emperors) Fasting observed by opera troupes. Since the first day to the ninth day of the first month of the Chinese lunar calendar, the troupe members would be dressed in white, burn incense praying, and offer sacrifices to Jiuhuang every day. On the evening of the ninth day, they would kowtow to the Nine Star Emperor, along with the Xuanwushan Buddha and Marshall Tian, the God of Opera. Some of the ordinary people worshipped Jiuhuang, too. Nevertheless, in Thailand, those overseas Chaozhou Chinese observe Jiuhuang Fasting strictly and solemnly. From the first day to the ninth day of the first month, they will fast for the sake of Jiuhuang and offer sacrifices to him, too. The Jiuhuang God they honor is different from the nine stars in the ancient Chinese mythology, from the Han people folklore, too, which says the worldly emperor had nine heads, and he had nine brothers who managed jiuzhou (nine parts of China). Instead, the Jiuhuang God they honored, originally nine thieves, later controlled by Bodhisattva, forsook the evil ways and returned to the right path. As a result, they became benevolent and pathetic, and had done a lot of good deeds. Thus they became the eldest disciple of the Buddha and worshipped by people. This is an evidence of different customs of overseas Chaoshan Chinese from the local ones in terms of the Double Ninth customs.

Since ancient times, people in Chaoshan area inherited the traditions of enjoying chrysanthemum, dining on chrysanthemum, drinking chrysanthemum wine, and wearing chrysanthemum, etc. The masterpiece of the traditional Chinese medicine, Shennong's Classic of Materia Medica, recorded that "Long-term taking of chrysanthemum has the following effects: stimulation of blood circulation, reducing weight, anti-aging, and longevity". Thus the ancient people prized chrysanthemum as "Longevity Elixir". The Chrysanthemum banquet is one of the unique local customs. It literally refers to the banquet of delicacies made of chrysanthemum. Some of them are as follows:

Chicken Soup with Chrysanthemum:

1. Rinse chrysanthemum petals and dry them, cut chicken into thin slices;

2. Prepared chicken (or chicken bone) soup;

3. Add vegetable oil and top-grade fish sauce into the soup;

4. When the soup is boiling, put the chicken slices into it;

5. After the chicken is done, sprinkle chrysanthemum petals into it and stir the soup.

Chicken is tender and tasty while chrysanthemum petals are fragrant. This delicacy, in Beijing, the capital city of the Qing Dynasty, is called "chrysanthemum hotpot", which is fragrant, tasty, and makes people mouth-watering.

Stir-Fried Shredded Pork with Chrysanthemum:

1. Rinse chrysanthemum petals, dry them and rip them off into shreds;

2. Cut choiced pork into chrysanthemum-shaped shreds and stir it with bean or sweet potato powder, salt and water;

3. Put the pot on the stove, fry shredded pork into white by using peanut oil, and then add top grade fish sauce;

4. Add chrysanthemum shreds and stir it.

The delicacy features its bright colors—yellow and white shreds, fragrant smell, and tender and slippery taste.

Shelled Shrimps with Chrysanthemum:

1. Cut the fresh shelled shrimps with one opening and clean them, but don't cut them into slices;

2. Cut spring onions and ginger into shreds; rinse yellow and white chrysanthemums;

3. Put the iron pot on the stove and fry shelled shrimps until they become red, and add fish sauce and vinegar into it;

4. Add shredded chrysanthemum, stir it.

The gourmets praise highly of this delicacy which features tender and slippery shelled shrimps, and fragrant and fresh chrysanthemum.

Steamed Perch with Chrysanthemum:

1. Choose the fresh autumn perch with tender and silver-white meat;

2. Scale the perch, cut open the belly, clean it, preserve it in

Shelled Shrimps with Chrysanthemum

145

salt, and dry it;

3. Cut red pepper and ginger into shreds, add soy sauce and stir them into seasonings;

4. Sprinkle the seasonings and chrysanthemum petals evenly on the perch;

5. Steam it for fifteen minutes by high heat.

The delicacy features bright color, tender taste, and fragrant smell.

Chrysanthemum Porridge:

1. Rinse rice of 100 grams, add water, and simmer it into porridge;

2. When the porridge is nearly sticky, add chrysanthemum of about 20 grams into it and stir it.

This porridge has the functions of cleaning liver, improving eyesight, anti-inflammation, stimulating blood circulation, reducing weight, and longevity.

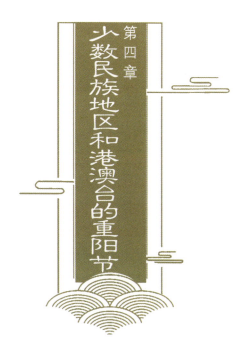

第四章 少数民族地区和港澳台的重阳节

在民族文化的相互交流过程中，中国少数民族地区的节日体系就逐渐地纳入了诸如春节、清明、端午、中秋等重大的汉文化节日。就重阳节来说壮族、毛南族、苗族、侗族等每年都会用自己的方式庆祝这一隆重的节日。

一、
少数民族的重阳节

　　在民族文化的相互交流过程中，中国少数民族地区的节日体系逐渐地融入了诸如春节、清明、端午、中秋等重大的汉文化节日。就重阳节来说壮族、毛南族、苗族、侗族等每年都会用自己的方式庆祝这一隆重的节日。

（一）壮族的"补粮"

　　在壮族地区，其重阳节有着"添寿"的习俗，一般是农历九月九日，有的地方也在农历十月十日进行（也有在"霜降"日）。壮族老人满60岁生日那天，儿孙为老人置一个寿粮缸。此后，农历十月十日（9月9日或"霜降"日）。晚辈都要给寿缸添粮，直到添满为止，就是出嫁的女儿也要在这天拎着新米回娘家"补粮缸"。这缸粮米称为"寿米"，只有老人病时方可食用。非老人自己，一般任何人无权私下处理"寿米"。

　　人上了年纪，生理功能衰减，免疫力差，头痛脑热是经常的事。德保、那坡、都安、巴马一带壮族先民认为，人活到五十岁，他命中注定的口粮已经吃完，已经到了大限。为增加寿命，必须给他添粮，向邻里亲戚借来"谷种"给他带来新的生命力，借助众人的"气势"维持以后的生命，延长寿命。因此，在四十九岁时，孝顺的子女就按照传统习惯给父母举办"添粮补寿"活动。

"补粮"要选择吉日举行，请道公根据老人的"生辰八字"，按五行生克的原理来确定"补粮"的日期。如：老人的生日属金，那就要选择土日来进行补粮，因为是土生金，用土来辅佐金的不足，使其金旺，以此类推。择定吉日后，孝主（老人的子女）即通知所有宗亲，包括已出嫁的女子，届时要全部出席补粮仪式。已出嫁的女儿、孙女要给老人准备寿衣、寿服、寿鞋等礼物，女婿、孙女婿还要给老人献上锦旗，上题"寿比南山"、"寿享遐龄"等祝寿用语。

"补粮"之日，孝主在房屋的中堂设置一张祭桌，摆上三碗大米当做香炉，分别插上奉请诸神牌位及受"补粮"老人的奏文，祭桌的四个脚上绑四根去枝留顶的青竹竿，每根竹竿分别挂上谷穗和布匹。祭桌旁边备有一箩筐大米，孝主所杀的牲头煮熟后全部端上祭桌供奉，道公宣布仪式开始后，孝主面对祭桌下跪，道公一边敲击小锣，一边念诵祷词。

在道公念诵祷词过程中，孝主分三次给祖先神位献酒献茶，当第三次献酒献茶结束后，受"补粮"的老人进入卧室坐在床沿上，双手拿一个红布袋。孝主手执黑色布匹，把一头放在祭桌旁的装有大米的箩筐内，再把另一头放在老人的怀里。当道公宣布给老人"补粮"时，到场参加仪式的子孙，排好队按次序一次一人到祭桌旁下跪，双手接过道公从箩筐里盛上的一碗米后，再拿出各自准备好的钱币（数目不限），放在米碗里，顺着这块黑布走到老人面前，恭恭敬敬地把米和钱装进老人手拿的红布袋，并说一些祝老人健康长寿的彩话，然后退出卧室。所有到场的人一一给老人补完粮后，道公切上

149

几块已煮熟了的肉和一碗饭送到老人床前，做上一段法事后，由孝主给老人喂食，然后道公将一条事先准备好的红布带系在老人的腰上，再把祭桌的四根青竹竿放到老人的床头或蚊帐上，封灯，燃放鞭炮，仪式结束。所有参加仪式的人上桌就餐，举杯祝福老人康宁长寿。子孙们给老人补上的这些钱和粮，日后由老人根据需要自行安排享用，不能送给第二者共享。

　　四根青竹杆之所以不能去顶，寓喻着老人的生命没有终点，永远蓬勃向上，所挂的谷穗寓意着一年四季不断粮，快乐平安，无灾无难，健康长寿。

○壮族补粮

　　"补粮"习俗，是壮族原始宗教在生活中的缩影，从表面形式上看，不免掺杂一些迷信色彩，但也体现出壮民族尊老爱老的道德风尚。给老人"补粮"，不仅是晚辈从物质上关心长辈，更重要的是给老人精神上的安慰，实质上起到了精神疗法的作用。心理上的健康可战胜生理上的不足，有句俗语说"有命不怕病"，这些受"补粮"过的老人，认为生命已得到延续，无忧无虑，愉快地生活，过好每一天。

　　"补粮"习俗是壮民族民俗文化与现代文明中多元而丰富的精神生活和谐相融的体现，这些原生态的民俗文化，已不再被简单地曲解为愚昧的产物，它渗透到人们的生活当中，成为不可或缺的精神食粮。这种精神陈酿，只有用心灵去面对去感悟，才能体察出它所释放出来的能量。

"添粮补命"也因此成为壮族一道独特的长寿文化风景线。

（二）毛南族的南瓜节

广西毛南族的南瓜节和重阳节的时节一致（农历九月九日），于是一起欢度。各家把收获到家的形状各异、桔黄色的大南瓜摆满楼板，逐一挑选。年轻人走门串户，到各家评选"南瓜王"。不仅要看外观，而且要凭经验透过表面看到瓜籽。待到众人意见基本一致，由一身强力壮者用砍刀劈开"南瓜王"，主人掏出瓜瓢，把饱满的籽留作来年的种子。然后把瓜切成块，放进小米粥锅里，文火煨炖，煮得烂熟，先盛一碗供在香火堂前敬奉"南瓜王"，然后众人共餐同享。

○广西毛南族南瓜节

151

中国许多民族把重阳节视为老人节，有敬老的传统习俗。毛南族也不例外，只是风尚不同。对于年过花甲而又体弱多病的老人，毛南人一般在重阳节时为之"添粮补寿"。子女们在这天置办几桌酒席于家中，请亲朋好友光临，来客都要带几斤细粮好米或者新鲜水果。亲友送来的"百家米"要单独贮存。日后在给老人做饭时抓一些掺进自家米中。"百家米"吃完了，老人若未康复，还得继续择日搞"添粮补寿"仪式。这种风俗实际上是出于对老人的一片爱心，很符合群众的道德及传统观念，得到当地政府的支持和重视。

背景知识

中国的毛南族

毛南族是中国人口较少的山地民族之一。毛南族自称"阿难"，意思是"这个地方的人"，称谓表明他们是岭西的土著民族。虽然毛南族人口较少，但他们却以悠久的历史和独特的文化闻名于世。毛南族主要分布在广西壮族自治区西北部的环江县，其余散居在南丹、河池、都安等地。毛南族地区紧靠云贵高原东麓，溶岩遍布，青山连绵。中部是茅南山，东北部是九万大山，西北部是凤凰山，西南部是大石山区，林木苍翠，属亚热带气候，适合于农耕畜牧。广西环江县的上南、中南、下南一带山区更是被称为"三南"，素有"毛南之乡"之称。

毛南族有自己的语言，属汉藏语系壮侗语族侗水语支。几乎所有毛南族人都兼通汉语和壮语。毛南族没有本民族文字，现通用汉文。唱歌是毛南族人最喜爱的文娱活动，民歌形式随编随唱，有昼夜连唱不停的才能。情歌叫"比"，祝贺歌谓"欢"，歌手称为"近比"、"近欢"。此外，还流行"毛南戏"。

毛南族主要经营农业、雕刻、编织竹器、牧养菜牛。木工、铁工等手工业、副业也占一定比重。特产是毛南菜牛。

（三）仫佬族重阳酒

重阳酒又称贵宾酒，亦称"吉祥酒"。重阳酒是苗族人和仫佬山乡农家最喜欢的传统饮料，是孝敬长辈、招待贵宾的上等饮品，故称"贵宾"：重阳酒，源远流长，历史悠久，晋代《抱朴子》记载，饮九九之重阳能延年益寿，直到明清，重阳酒仍是盛行的健身饮料，是重阳必饮之酒，据传记，喝重阳酒具有驱风避邪、祛灾祈福的神效，所以又称"吉祥酒"。

仫佬山乡被一些有钱人霸占了，广大的幺佬人贫穷困苦，日艰月难。重阳节到来了，一对在山窝里开荒种地，相依为命的穷苦夫妻，没鸡没鸭，没肉没酒，只有半缸底米，只好熬了三碗稀粥过节。他们夫妻俩各自吃了一碗后，正在你推我让，谁也舍不得吃的时候，传来了敲门声。他俩开门一看，门外站着一个白发苍苍、衣衫破烂的老人。夫妻俩问道："老人家，你有什么事呀？"老人说："主人家，我走远路经过这里，身无分文，已经三天都没有吃东西了。好心的人呀，能给我一点儿东西充充饥吗？"夫妻俩赶忙把老人请进屋里坐下，把那碗舍不得吃的稀粥端给老人吃。"老人家呀，真对不起你了，今天是重阳节，我们家穷，只有这碗粥了，你若不嫌弃，将就吃吧！"那老人也不客气，一口气就把粥喝光了。老人暖和过来后，对夫妻俩说："谢谢你们了，我教给你们一种酿酒的方法吧！"于是，他把重阳酒的酿制方法教给了夫妻俩，然后告诫说："这种酒千万千万不能卖呵！"说完，就不见了。第二年重阳节到了，夫妻俩按照老人说的方法酿制出一种酒。这种酒真奇怪，留久了不但没有像别的酒那样变酸，反而越陈越香甜。打开酒坛，满屋子飘香。喝上一口，隔几夜嘴巴还留香。夫妻俩高兴极了，把这种酿酒方法告诉乡亲们。这样，仫佬山乡家家都喝上了神仙美酒。因为神仙交待过这种酒是不能卖的，因而市面上没有卖的。

○仫佬山乡

　　仫佬山重阳酒是以苗乡的优质香糯米、泉水、甜酒曲等为原料，运用元宝山苗族小缸家酿的传统工艺及现代科学技术精心配制而成，并长时间密封窖藏于古老深洞之中，其越陈越香甜，在苗族之乡具有"香醇柔和"之美称，被誉为重阳酒的酒中上品。它具有十分浓厚的民族特色，具有家酿糯精甜酒的品味，口感怡人，香醇甜美，风味独特，真可谓"打开酒坛，满屋飘香，喝上一口，昼夜留香。"每年农历九月初九重阳节，幺佬山乡家家户户选出一部分上好的糯米熬酒。

　　重阳酒也是侗族人在重阳节时为重大节日准备的，当然也拿来

待客，但得是尊贵的客人
或情深意重的友人，所以
不是轻易能喝到的，就是
为人熟知的拦路酒也只是
包谷酒。重阳酒是鲜为人
知的、真正的深闺美人。
重阳酒的难得主要是因为
制作量少和制作时间长。
用的材料也是糯米，但必
须是深山里养育的，刚出
田的新鲜糯米，所用的水
得是山泉水。洒了山泉的
糯米饭拌酒曲发酵一个礼

○重阳酒

拜后，才开始蒸酒，蒸好的酒和甜酒糟放进坛子里密封上，最后要
在牛圈里挖个坑，把酒坛埋在牛粪土底下，至少要埋一年，当然埋
得越久越好，把酒糟都化了才好。

（四）土家族打糍粑

　　土家族世居湘、鄂、渝、黔毗连的武陵山区。土家族北支（湖南
省湘西州，张家界市以及湖北省恩施州、宜昌市的五峰、长阳，渝东南，
贵州黔东北）自称"毕兹卡、毕基卡、密基卡等等"。南支土家族仅
分布于湖南湘西州泸溪县内的几个村落，自称"孟兹"，南支土家
语与北部土家语不能通话，现只有泸溪的九百余人使用。土家语属
汉藏语系藏缅语族、土家语支，也有人认为应归入缅彝语支，是藏
缅语族内一种十分古老独特的语言。绝大多数人通晓汉语，如今只

155

有为数不多的几个聚居区还保留着土家语。土家族没有本民族文字，现时使用 1984 年创制的拉丁文字，通用汉文，崇拜祖先，信仰多神。

中国的传统节日——重阳节也是土家族的重要节日之一。每逢重阳节，家家都要打糯米糍粑。在土家族有一种"二十八，打粑粑"的说法。糍粑就是用糯米做成的类似年糕的食物，贵州、云南、四川等地称为糍粑。据乡土志书记载："米饭就石槽中杆如泥，压成团型，形如满月。"打糍粑是一项劳动强度较大的体力活，两个人对站，先揉后打。土家族人做糍粑的工序也很讲究，先用手蘸蜂蜡或茶油，之后搓涂，稍后用手或木板压，打糍粑务必要做得光滑、美观。

○土家族打糍粑（乡里乡亲们 摄）

二、
港澳台地区的重阳节

　　港澳台地区亦属于中国东南沿海，重阳节的习俗与相邻的省份习俗很接近。

　　据史料记载，香港重九祭祖的习俗，源自在新界最早定居的大族之一的上水乡廖族。廖族时至今日仍然保留此习俗，其秋祭的场面甚为浩大。不过，在参与人数和祭祀形式及规模方面，均有别于新界原居民以族为单位的祭祖活动。族人一般都带备烧猪、三牲酒礼及碗筷、杯盘、镰刀等用具。抵达祖坟时，部分人取石堆砌炉灶，准备传统的盘菜，另一部分人则清理坟旁杂草，扫除垃圾。

　　重阳拜山是香港人由来已久的风俗。在秋祭正日，族长、二族、房长、父老（六十一岁或以上的男性族人）、乡绅及其他宗族成员，联同凤溪学校员生列队前往先人墓地拜祭。当所有人到达仲杰公墓，族中负责祭祀仪式的通赞便会安排参拜者根据辈分的高低就列于祖坟前，准备拜祭。首先燃放爆竹，然后奏乐，接着参拜者行三叩首之礼，之后由族长奠酒，献香烛及祭品。在宣读祝文后，各乡绅依辈分次序奠祭。礼成后，辈分较高的族人可领取胙肉一份，当地人称之为"太公分猪肉"。在农业社会，猪肉是一种贵重的食物。故此，"太公分猪肉"

这一仪式可反映出宗族对辈分的重视及礼遇。虽然猪肉已变成很普通的食物，但它的象征意义并没有因此而改变。

此外，重阳节时，香港市民或举家登高，或扫墓祭祖。由于香港的主要墓园都在山上，扫墓的同时也实现了登高，颇切合时节。资料记载，新界原乡民重九祭祖，通常分为三次：第一次是私人扫墓，即小家庭式祭祖；第二次是房份扫墓，由数家至十余家人不等；第三次是大众扫墓，即全村同姓，无论已迁出或分居各地都共同祭祖，结队前往扫墓。重阳祭祖者比清明为多，故俗有以三月为小清明，重九为大清明之说。由于莆仙沿海，九月初九也是妈祖羽化升天的忌日，乡民多到湄洲妈祖庙或港里的天后祖祠、宫庙祭祀，求得保佑。

○香港平地很少，主要墓园几乎都在山上

台湾也有过重阳节的习俗，高拱干《台湾府志·卷七》中记载：重阳节时，士大夫们都会带着酒登高聚会，台湾当地的菊花开得早，重阳节时，盛开的菊花数不胜数。可见台湾过重阳习俗和中国各地几乎是一样的。

台湾的气候自九月开始就刮起了号称"九降"的秋风，吹的是无雨的北风，此时最适宜放风筝。胡建伟《澎湖纪略·卷七》上记载了放风筝的情形：风筝的形状多种多样，有人物状、凤凰状等，形形色色。它们迎风飞舞，晚上把灯系在上面，就像夜空中的星星一样璀璨。这时候，还会一起比赛，风筝放得高的为胜者。另俗话说的："九月九，风吹（风筝）满天哮。"说的也是重阳风筝满天飞的盛况。放风筝时不仅外形争奇斗艳，还以"风吹相咬"（就是玩风筝"打架"）为乐事。好斗者往往会在风筝上加装暗器，如小锯片或尖锐的铅片等，用来切断对方的丝线，或者是放长丝线去缠拉大风筝的尾巴，然后再用力一扯就将大风筝拉下来了。如果不幸风筝被扯下坠地，也往往成了众人抢夺的目标。战败者会以"风吹断了线，家伙（财产）去了一半。"来形容自己的损失惨重。台湾客家族群，也有在重阳节祭祖的习俗，而以头份东庄里诸家族的祭祖活动最为热闹盛大。传说东庄里有钟、饶两大姓氏，原本在唐山祖籍时就是邻居。乾隆年间来台后，也把重阳祭祖习俗带了过来。后来叶姓家族也加入重阳祭祖活动，庄中其他姓氏族人觉得不能年年让这三姓族人宴请，慢慢也加入重阳祭祖的活动了。据说祭祖时越早到越能得到祖先的庇佑。

IV

The Double Ninth Festival in Ethnic Minority Regions & in Hong Kong and Macao,and Taiwan

缺辑页英文

1. The Double Ninth Festival in Ethic Minority Regions

In the mutual communication between ethnic groups, the festivals in ethnic minority inhabitations have gradually absorbed the major Han festivals, such as the Spring Festival, Tomb Sweeping Festival, Dragon Boat Festival, and Mid-Autumn Festival, etc. As for the Double Ninth Festival, the ethnic minority people like Zhuang, Maonan, Miao, and Dong observe it in a solemn way.

Buniang (Adding Grain) of Zhuang

In Autonomous Region of Zhuang, there's the custom of "Tianshou (Adding Longevity)", which generally falls on the ninth day of the ninth month or the tenth day of the tenth month (or on the solar term "Frost's Descent") in the Chinese lunar calendar. On the day when Zhuang people gets 60 years old, his children and grandchildren will buy a Longevity Grain Jar. Since then, on every ninth day of the ninth month or the tenth day of the tenth month, his descendants will add grain to the jar until it's full, even his married daughters will come back home for doing so. This jar of grain is called "Longevity Grain", which can only be taken by the seniors when they're sick. No other people have the right to handle with it unless the seniors, themselves.

It's unavoidable for seniors to get sick with the decline of their health. The ancestors of Zhuang people in Debao, Napo, Du'an, and Bama counties in Guangxi Province thought one would run out of the grain in all his life and his life would come to an end when he gets fifty. To prolong his life, his children will add grain to the Longevity Grain Jar, even borrow grain from their neighbors and relatives to instill new vigor into his life. Therefore, the filial children will hold the ceremony of "Adding Grain for Longevity" for their parents.

"Adding Grain" will be held on an auspicious day when the Daogong (Taoist Priest) was asked for deciding the day for this ceremony based on his birthday and following the generative or destructive relations between the five elements of the world, metal, wood, water, fire, and earth ; for example, if the senior's birthday is of metal nature, the day of earth would be chosen because according to the traditional Chinese medicine and ancient Chinese philosophy, earth fosters metal and it's necessary to use earth for complementing the deficiency of the metal and nourishing it. After the auspicious day was chosen, the senior's children would notice all relatives of their big family, including the married daughters, for attending the ceremony. The married daughters and granddaughters were expected to prepare longevity costume and shoes for the senior while his son-in-laws and grandson-in-laws for dedicating silk banner which writes "寿比南山" (shou bi nan shan; living as long as the South Mountain) and "寿享遐龄" (shou xiang xia ling; wishing longevity), etc.

On the Adding Grain Day, the senior's children set a table in the middle of the living room with three big bowls of rice as incense burners, into which the tablets of gods and the prayers

162

for the senior were stuck. Four bamboo poles with leaves were bound around the four table legs, each of them being hung with yellow grains and cloth. There was a large bamboo basket of rice beside the table. The heads of the livestock were stewed and served on the table as sacrifices. After Daogong declared the commencement of the ceremony, the seniors' children knelt in front of the table while the former beat the drum and prayed.

While Daogong prayed, the senior's children dedicated wine and tea to the tablets of ancestors for three times. Then, the senior entered his living room and sat on the bed with a red cloth bag in his two hands. His children took a black cloth with one end in the rice basket and another tucked in the senior's clothes. As soon as Daogong declared "Add Grain", the children knelt down one by one in front of the table, respectively took a bowl of rice from him, took out money and put them into the rice bowl. Then they, following the black cloth, approached the senior, put the rice and money into his red bag and wished him health and longevity before they retreated from the bedroom. After all of the children added grain to the senior, Daogong would serve several cubes of pork and a bowl of rice to the senior and practise some religious rites. Then, the children would feed the senior, and Daogong would bind a prepared red cloth around his waist and put the four bamboo poles on his bed or his mosquito net, turning off the lights and lighting firecrackers. The whole ceremony was ended in this way. All the attendants would dine and wished the senior health and longevity. No other person but the senior himself can handle with the money and rice added by the children.

The four green bamboo poles cannot be cut off the heads, which implies that the senior's life is endless and thriving; the yellow grains stand for adequate food, happiness, peace, health, and longevity.

The custom of Adding Grain, a mirror of the primitive religion of Zhuang people, superficially, being superstitious, fully demonstrates their fine tradition of revering and loving seniors. Adding Grain to seniors not only give them material support, but more importantly, mental comfort, actually being a kind of mental therapy. As a matter of fact, mental health surpasses physical health since an old saying goes "Those blessed are not afraid of illness". The seniors who go through

Zhuang People Adding Grain for Seniors

Adding Grain ceremony are encouraged to believe that their lives have been lengthened and can live carefree every day.

The custom of Adding Grain integrates the ancient Zhuang ethnic folk customs with diversified modern ways of living. The original folk cultures have been infiltrated into people's lives and become an indispensable part of them instead of being regarded as consequence of ignorance.

"Adding Grain for Longevity" has become a spectacular cultural phenomenon in Zhuang people.

Pumpkin Festival of Maonan Ethic Group

The Pumpkin Festival of Maonan people falls on the same day as the Double Ninth Festival does. So they spend the two festivals on the same day. People exhibit the orange pumpkins on the floor. The young people visit every household for choosing "The King of Pumpkin" and they must have the capacity of seeing seeds through the skin of the pumpkins. When people see eye to eye with each other, a strong man will be singled out to split the King of Pumpkin into two halves whose seeds are chosen for next year's sowing. Then, the pumpkin will be chopped into cubes and simmered with millet. A bowl of pumpkin and millet porridge will be served as sacrifices to the King of Pumpkin. Finally people will share the porridge together.

Many ethnic groups regard the Double Ninth Festival as the Seniors' Festival, which represents their tradition of revering the seniors. Maonan people are no exception, but they observe it in different ways. For those seniors who are above 60 years old, sick and weak, they will Add Grain for them. The seniors' children will treat at home their relatives and friends who will bring with them some quality rice or fresh fruits. The Hundred Family Rice brought by the relatives or friends will be stored alone for being added into daily rice cooking. If the Hundred Family Rice runs out but the seniors have not recovered yet, another Adding Grain ceremony will be held. This kind of custom demonstrates local people's affection for seniors, which conforms to people's moral and traditional values and is prized by the local government.

Background information

Maonan Ethnic Group of China

The Maonan nationality is an ethnic group who lives in the mountain with a small fraction of population. They call themselves "A'Nan", which means "people in this place". This addressing indicates that they're aboriginals of this place. Although the population is small, they're famous for their long history and unique culture. They mainly live in the Huangjiang County, north–west of Guangxi Zhuang Autonomous Region and the rest of them scatter in Nandan, Hechi, and Du'an. The Maonan people inhabitation, being close to the east slope of the Yungui Plateau, features eroded caves and lush green mountains. In the middle part of the habitation is the Maonan Mountain, to its north-east is the Nine Thousand Mountains, and to its south-west is the Big Rock Mountains. The mountains, positioned in the sub–tropical climate area, are covered with green trees and meadow, suitable for agriculture and livestock husbandry.

Upper South, Middle South, and Lower South areas in Huangjiang County are briefed as "Three South Area", the origin of Maonan.

Maonan people have their own languages, classified as Dongshui branch, Zhuang and Dong phylum, Sino-Tibetan language family. Almost all of them are good at using Chinese and Zhuang Language. They don't have their written language and adopt Chinese as their script. Singing is their most favorite recreational activity. They can compose songs whenever they'd like to and can keep singing for several days on end. The love songs are Bi, songs for congratulations are Huan , and correspondingly the singers are "Jin Bi" and "Jin Huan". In addition, the Maonan Opera is popular, too.

The Maonan people mainly go in for farming, engravings, bamboo weaving, and raising beef cattle. Some people are carpenters and smiths. The local specialty is Maonan beef cattle.

Double Ninth Wine of Mulao Ethnic Group

The Double Ninth Wine is also called Distinguished Guest Wine or Auspicious Wine. The Double Ninth Wine is the most favorable traditional drinking of Miao and Mulao people as well as the top drinking dedicated to seniors and distinguished guests, hence the name Distinguished Guest Wine. It boasts a long history. As early as in the Jin Dynasty, the well-known Taoist and doctor Ge Hong wrote in his works The Master of Preserving Simplicity : drinking the Double Ninth Wine was effective in anti-aging and keeping healthy. Even in the Ming and Qing Dynasties, the Double Ninth Wine was popular health drinking, which could dispel evil wind and ward off evil spirits as well as escaping disasters and praying for blessing, hence the name "Auspicious Wine".

The tale goes like the following: Long long ago, the Mulao inhabitation was occupied by wealthy people while the ordinary Mulao people were poverty-stricken and had difficult times. On one Double Ninth Festival, a poor farmer couple who tilled the soil in the deep mountains had nothing but only half jar of rice, so they only made three bowls of porridge for celebrating it. The couple loved each other so much that they'd like to leave the last bowl of porridge for each other after they had one bowl each. At this moment came the knock on the door. They opened the door and found an old man with gray hair and ragged clothes. They asked: "What's wrong with you?" The old man answered, "I wandered in the wild for three days but had nothing to eat. Would you please be so kind to give me some food?" The couple immediately let him in, had him seated, and served him the last bowl of porridge by saying: "We're so sorry that there's only this left because we're poor. Please have it if you'd like to." The old man said nothing and swallowed it within one stroke. After he warmed up, he said to the couple: "For expressing my gratitude, I will teach you how to make wine". So he taught the recipe of making the Double Ninth Wine to them and warned them never to sell it. Then he was gone. On the next Double Ninth Festival, the couple made wine by following the old man's mystery. The wine became more and more fragrant with the time passing by instead of becoming sour. Taking off the lid of the jar, it smells fragrantly in the whole room. Taking a sip of it and fragrance stayed for several days. The couple was thrilled and told the recipe to their country fellows. In this way, the Mulao people got access to the fine wine; however, it was not available in the market according to the warning of the immortal.

The Double Ninth Wine of the Mulao Mountain is made of quality glutinous rice, spring water, and sweet wine yeast made in Miao people's small family-brewed wine jar by combining modern technology. Since it's tightly sealed and stored in the ancient cellar deeply underground, the longer it's brewed, the more fragrant it is. It's crowned as top Double Ninth wine owing to its mellow and soft taste. Taking off the lid of the jar, it smells fragrantly in the whole room. Taking a sip of it and fragrance stayed for several days. On every Double Ninth Festival, the Mulao mountain villagers will choose some quality glutinous rice for brewing wine.

The Double Ninth Wine is prepared for the festive occasion as well as treating distinguished guests and intimate friends. Even the well-known Welcoming Wine is made of corn. The value of the Double Ninth Wine lies in its scarcity and long time of brewing. The ingredients must be newly-reaped glutinous rice which grows in the deep mountains, and spring water in the deep mountains, too. The glutinous cooked rice sprinkled with mountain spring water will be set for a week after yeast being added. A week later, the steamed wine with the sweet distiller's grains will be filled into the jar tightly

169

sealed. Of course, the longer it's brewed, the better it is.

Glutinous rice paste of Tujia ethnic group

The Tujia ethnic group inhabits in the Wuling Mountains located in Hunan, Hubei, Sichuan, and Guizhou provinces. They call themselves Bizika which means Bizi Clan (ka has the meaning of ancestors). The north clan of Tujia people, who live in the Xiangxi Miao and Tujia Autonomous Region (west of Hunan Province), the Enshi Miao and Tujia Autonomous Region, Wufeng County, Changyang County of Hubei Province, south-east of Sichuan, and north-east of Guizhou, calls themselves Bizika, Bijika, or Mijika. The south clan, who lives in several villages in Luxi County of the Xiangxi Miao and Tujia Autonomous Region, having only about 900 people, calls themselves Mengzi and has their own language which cannot be understood by the north clan. Tujia language belongs to

Tujia People Pounding Glutinous Rice Paste (by Fellow Countrymen)

Glutinous Rice Paste of Tujia People

Bermese and Yi (another two ethnic groups in China) branch or Tujia branch, Tibetan and Burmese Phylum, Sino-Tibetan language family. It's a special kind of ancient language. The majority of Tujia people understand Chinese while only several inhabitations adopt Tujia language. They don't have their own written language, either, and adopt Chinese as their script. They worship ancestors and believe in multiple deities.

The Double Ninth Festival, a traditional festival of Chinese, is also one of the major festivals for Tujia people. On the Double Ninth Festival, every family will make Glutinous Rice Paste (People in Guizhou, Yunan, Sichuan, and partially in Hubei and Hunan call it Ciba while otherwise named Niangao, glutinous rice cake). According to the local chronicles, "The local people put the steamed glutinous rice into the stone mortar, pounded with a pestle until it was mashed, pressed it into circular shape as a full moon." Pounding Glutinous Rice Paste is a kind of strong manual labor with two people standing by facing each other, kneading the rice first and then pounding it in turn. Tujia people are very particular about making Rice Paste: they dip their fingers into beewax or tea-seed oil first and rub their hands with it, and then press the rice paste with their hands or a wooden board until it is smooth and attractive in appearance.

2. The Double Ninth Festival in Hong Kong, Macao, and Taiwan

Hong Kong, Macao, and Taiwan are located in south-east coast of China. The customs of spending the Double Ninth Festival of local people are close to those of their neighboring mainland provinces.

According to history, the Hong Kong customs of spending the Double Ninth Festival originated from the Liao Family of Shangshui Village, who was earliest settlers in the New Territories and one of the big clans there. The Liao Family still keeps the grand autumn sacrifice; however, the number of attendants, way of offering sacrifices, and the scale of the occasion have all changed, which is different from the original tradition of worshipping ancestors on the basis of family clan. The people of the same clan prepare roast pig and other livestock, wine, and gifts as well as food ware and sickles in advance. When they arrive at their ancestors' cemeteries, some of them make stove with rocks and make dishes whereas others clean the grass and garbage on and around the tombs.

Worshipping mountain is a tradition of Hong Kong people. On the day of autumn sacrifice, the clan head, the family heads, and patriarchal seniors (male clan members of or above 61 years old), squires, and other clan members, along with the students of the Fengxi School, went to their ancestors' cemetery for worshipping. When all of them arrived at the cemetery, the chief-in-sacrifice will let the attendants queue up in front of the ancestors' tombs by virtue of seniority within the family generational hierarchy. Then firecrackers were set, music was played, and the attendants kowtowed for three times. The clan head offered wine to the ancestors, lit candles and burnt incense, and offered other sacrifices. After the prayer was read, the squires offered sacrifices one by one on the basis

Cemetery of Hong Kong on the top of Mountains

of seniority. After the ceremony was over, the members with higher seniority could claim a strip of sacrifice pork, which was called "Grand-grand-pa Distributing Pork". In the agricultural society, pork is a precious kind of gift. Therefore, Grand-grand-pa Distributing Pork reflected that seniority had been given priority to by a clan. Although pork is not precious any more, its symbolic meaning hasn't changed.

Apart from that, on the Double Ninth Festival, the Hong Kong people ascend the height or sweep the tombs for honoring ancestors. Owing to the fact that the cemeteries in Hong Kong are generally located on the top of mountains, these two rituals can be practiced at the same time. According to the recording, the aboriginals of the New Territories used to honor their ancestors for three times on the Double Ninth Festival. The first is sweeping tombs of each core family. The second is that on the basis of big family. Several or scores of families sweep tombs together. The third is that of mass, i.e., the people with the same surname in one village, no matter they're still in or outside of the village, go for honoring their ancestors together. Actually, there're more people who honor ancestors on the Double Ninth Festival than those on the Tomb Sweeping Festival. That's why people call the former one bigger Tomb Sweeping Festival while the latter smaller one.

People in Taiwan also observe the customs of the Double Ninth Festival. The Chronicles of Taiwan, Volume Seven by Gao Gonggan recorded that: on the Double Ninth Festival, officials and men of letters ascended the height by bringing with them wine for gathering. The chrysanthemums of Taiwan bloom earlier than those in the mainland. Taiwan people can generally have the similar festive activities as those in other places of China.

Since Sep., the autumn wind named "Nine Descends" prevails in Taiwan, i.e., the northern wind which doesn't carry rain. So it's the best time for kite-flying. The Chronicles of Penghu, Volume Seven by Hu Jianwei recorded flying-kite during that time: kites feature its varied shapes, of figures, of phoenix, etc. They danced in the sky by braving the wind. If tied with lights, they would glitter like stars in the night sky. There was kite race, too. The highest kite would be rewarded. Just as the old saying said: "On the ninth day of the ninth month, wind blowing kites high, and kites howling in the sky". People not only competed against each other by virtue of kites' shape or color, they but also had great fun in mutual biting of kites (kites were entangled with each other and struggled with each other). They would equip kites with "hidden weapons", such as small saw blades or sharp lead sheet, to cut off the rival kites' string, or lengthen the string of their own kites to entangle the rival kites' tail and pulled them down with strength. If some kite dropped, people would swarm to pick it. The loser would sneer themselves by saying "Kite string was broken and half of my fortune was broken, too" to describe his great loss. The Hakka people in Taiwan observed the ritual of honoring ancestors, too, on the Double Ninth Festival. The grandest ceremony was held by the several families in DongZhuangli Village of Miaoli County. The tale had that there were two big families, with the surname of Zhong and Rao, respectively, who were neighbors when they were living in Tangshan, a northern city of China mainland. After they moved to Taiwan during the reign of the Emperor Qianlong, they brought with them the customs of honoring ancestors. Later, the Ye family joined in the ceremony and the other families joined it in, too, since they felt it improper to be always treated by the three big families annually. It was said: the earlier to honor ancestors, the earlier to be blessed by them.

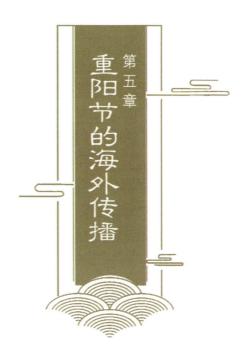

第五章

重阳节的海外传播

以节日习俗而言，重阳节虽然发源地在中国，但是在长期的流传和国际交流中，它已经被中国周边的国家和民族所吸纳、所接受，并被置于他们自己的文化土壤之中，形成了周边国家民族独特的节日习俗。其中，最具代表性的是韩国和日本的重阳节。

一、
韩国重阳节

在韩国，农历九月九日叫重九，是有名的节日之一。重九不仅在阴阳哲学上有着重要的意义，而且也是象征丰收到来的节日，因而历来都是很受追捧的传统节日。从新罗时代开始就有在重九这天在月上楼聚会吟诗的风俗。到了高丽时代，重九的享宴甚至成了带有国家性质的惯例，成为内外大臣和宋朝、耽罗、黑水的远客一起参加祝贺的宴会。在朝鲜时代的世宗时把重三、重九定为节日，甚至把在中秋节时开的耆老宴也改在重九这一天进行。因它有长久之意，所以常在此日祭祖与推行敬老活动。通常，重阳节这天会喝菊花酒、吃菊花饼、栗子糕、菊花煎庆祝节日。通过和家人分享这些应景的食品，一起登上

○韩国菊花糕

多彩中国节

重阳节

首尔的南山或者北汉山又吃又喝地度过一天，是韩国人在重阳这天的传统风俗。

重阳节不止是赏菊的好日子，也是枫叶红了的时节，所以为了观赏枫叶，人们会从很远的地方来看枫叶，逍遥自在，这就是："消枫"。一词的由来。在首尔的近郊区，景致绝妙的山和山沟很多，选择在重阳这天登高远眺，既能陶冶身心，又能欣赏美景哦！

○ 菊花煎

二、
日本重阳节

日本有"五大节日"，分别是指公历 1 月 7 日人日（吃七草粥），3 月 3 日女儿节，5 月 5 日端午节，7 月 7 日七夕节以及 9 月 9 日重阳节。在中国古代，人们认为奇数是代表美好事物的阳数，偶数是代表不

179

好事物的阴数，而庆祝连续奇数的日子就成了五大节日的起源。其中 9 月 9 日是最大的阳数 9 碰在一起，就写作"重叠的阳"，并命名为"重阳节"，举行祈求长生不老和子孙繁荣的庆祝活动。民间还有用菊花维持少年的样貌，活了 700 年的"菊慈童"的传说。

如今重阳节在五大节日中的地位已经淡薄了，但在以前，作为五大节日的总结仪式，其庆祝的仪式是最盛大的。五大节日经常被冠以与之相关的植物名字来称呼，3 月 3 日又叫桃子节，5 月 5 日是菖蒲节，7 月 7 日是细竹节，而 9 月 9 日被叫做菊花节。在日本平安时代初期，重阳节作为贵族的宫廷活动被引进到日本。随着时代的推移，重阳节从贵族社会扩展到武士和平民阶层。

在平安时代以前，秋收之际，农村、山村以及老百姓之间会过一种叫"栗子节"的节日，用栗子饭来庆祝。进入平安时期后，日本开始举办菊花宴，对饮菊花泡的"菊酒"，插上茱萸驱除邪气。另外还会举行与菊花有关的赛歌会和现在所说的"赛菊会"。

○日本京都的上贺茂神社

受了中国影响，日本人在 9 月 8 日的夜里在菊花上盖上棉花，第二天用被露水打湿的棉花擦拭身体以此祈求长寿。另外，还会举办一些与菊花相关的赛歌会或赏菊会。现在，这种活动越来越少，一般只在寺庙等地方进行。

　　在京都的上贺神社里现在还会举行祈求无病消灾的重阳节会。9 月 9 日那天，两名手持弓箭的刀弥，从镜内细殿前的相扑台左右两侧横跳出，出现在两堆沙堆前，嘴里模仿着鸟叫发出"咔——咔——咔"、"扩——扩——扩"的声音，然后附近的孩子会进行鸟相扑和棉盖菊的祭神仪式。在长崎，重阳节是充满异国情调的节庆，起源于两位艺妓在神前表演的舞曲，距今已经有 370 余年的历史。活动从 9 月 7 日开始，分 3 天举行。

V

The Overseas Communication of the Double Ninth Festival

Although the Double Ninth Festival originated in China, it has been accepted and absorbed by its neighboring countries, deeply rooted in their own cultures, and hence their own peculiar festive traditions have taken shape, among which, the most representative are those of South Korea and Japan.

1. The Double Ninth Festival in South Korea

In South Korea, the Double Ninth Festival falls on the ninth day of the ninth month in South Korean calendar. Since it is not only of significance in terms of philosophy of Yin and Yang, it but also stands for the coming of harvest, it's a highly-honored festival in South Korea. Since the Silla Era, the South Korean people had the custom of ascending the tower for gathering and writing poems. In the Koryo Era, the feast of the Double Ninth Festival had become a state routine, which the South Korean officials and the guests from Tamna (today's Cheju Island of South Korea) and the Heishui State (black water state, located in today's Zhangye City of Ganshu Province) attended. During the reign of the King of Sejong (1418—1450) in the history of South Korea, the government set the Double Third day and Double Ninth day as official holidays and moved the Seniors' Feast originally on the Mid-Autumn Day to the Double Ninth Festival. Due to the implication

Chrysanthemum Jelly of South Korea

183

of longevity contained in Double Ninth, South Korea promoted activities of revering seniors on this day, too. Usually the South Korean people drink chrysanthemum wine, have chrysanthemum jelly, chestnut cake, and pan-fried chrysanthemum cake for celebrating the Double

Pan-fried Chrysanthemum Cake

Ninth Festival. They'll bring these foods with them and climb the Namsan Mountain or the Bukaksan Mountain of Seoul, which is the tradition of South Korean people on the Double Ninth Festival.

On the Double Ninth Festival, chrysanthemum blooms in its prime and the maple leaves become red, too. People will come to enjoy maple leaves and relax from distant places. In the suburb of Seoul, there're quite a number of mountains and valleys with splendid sceneries. Ascending the height for looking into distance on the Double Ninth Festival is not only pleasing to your eyes but also cultivating your mind.

2. The Double Ninth Festival in Japan

There're five major festivals in Japan. They're respectively as follows: The Day of Human on Jan. 7th (The Japanese people will have seven vegetable porridge), the Girls' Festival on Mar. 3rd, the Dragon Boat Festival on May 5th, the Star Festival on July 7th, and the Double Ninth Festival on Sep. 9th. In ancient China, people thought the odd number was of Yang, standing for good luck and prosperity while the even number was of Yin, for bad luck and deterioration. Accordingly, the five major festivals fall on the days with double odd numbers, among which, the Double Ninth Festival falls on the ninth day of the ninth month, containing two biggest single-digit odd numbers "nine". Hence, it's appropriate for holding folk ceremonies of praying for longevity and prosperity of family.

Currently the Double Ninth Festival declines among the five major festivals of Japan. But before that, as the last one of the five major festivals, the Double Ninth Festival was celebrated with the grandest ceremony. The five major festivals in Japan have got additional names by associating them with plants; for example, the Double Third Day is called the Peach Festival, the Double Fifth Day the Calamus Festival, the Double Seventh Day the Fine Bamboo Festival, and the Double Ninth Day the Chrysanthemum Festival. At the beginning of the Heian Era of Japan, the Double Ninth Festival was introduced to Japan as a court ceremony. With the time passing by, it was extended from the aristocracy to warriors and common people.

Before the Heian Era, farmers, villagers and other ordinary people would spend the Chestnut Festival during the autumn harvest. They made chestnut rice for celebrating the festival. In the Heian Era, Japan began to host chrysanthemum feast, drinking chrysanthemum wine, and wearing Zhuyu for warding off evil spirits. Besides, singing race and chrysanthemum race were hosted, too.

Influenced by Chinese people, Japanese people would cover cotton on chrysanthemum on the eve of the Double Ninth Festival and used dew-moistened cotton for rubbing body the next day for praying for longevity.

Nevertheless, the above activities are seldom held and will be held in temples, generally.

The Double Ninth Festival Fair is still held in the Shinto Shrine, Kyoto, Japan for guarding off evil spirits and keeping

Shinto Shrine of Kyoto, Japan

healthy. On the Double Ninth day, two monks with archery jumped out respectively from the left and right side of the sumo stage and landed on the pile of sand by imitating the crowing of birds, ka-ka-ka and kuo-kuo-kuo. Then the nearby children will perform sumo and cover cotton on chrysanthemum. In Nagasaki, the Double Ninth Festival bears strong exotic flavor, originating from two geishas' dancing in front of deities, and enjoys the history of more than 370 years. The celebrations start from Sep. 7th and will last for three days.

附 录 Appendix:

"菊花酒"的酿制方法
Recipe of Brewing Chrysanthemum Wine

　　菊花酒由菊花与糯米、酒曲酿制而成的酒，古称"长寿酒"，其味清凉甜美，有养肝、明目、健脑、延缓衰老等功效。有枸杞菊花酒，花糕菊花酒，还有白菊花酒。重阳佳节，中国有饮菊花酒的传统习俗。菊花酒，在古代被看作是重阳必饮、祛灾祈福的"吉祥酒"。其酿制步骤如下：

Chrysanthemum wine is made of glutinous rice, chrysanthemum, and distiller's yeast. It has been called Longevity Wine by Chinese people. It tastes cool, sweet, and refreshing and has the functions of nourishing the liver, brightening the eyes, strengthening the brain, and anti-aging. There're chrysanthemum and wolfberry wine, rice cake and chrysanthemum wine, and white chrysanthemum wine. On the Double Ninth Festival, Chinese people observes the tradition of drinking chrysanthemum wine, which was regarded as auspicious wine for warding off evil spirits and praying for blessings. Here's the recipe:

多彩中国节

重阳节

材料：
主料：菊花 2000 克、稻米 3000 克
辅料：生地黄 1000 克、当归 500 克、
枸杞子 500 克
The main ingredients:
2000 grams of chrysanthemum
3000 grams of glutinous rice
The minor ingredients:
1000 grams of unprocessed rehmannia
root
500 grams of Chinese angelica
500 grams of Chinese wolfberry

制作步骤 / Procedures

1. 甘菊花，当归，生地黄入锅中，加水煎汁，用纱布过滤待用。
1. Put chrysanthemum, Chinese angelica, and unprocessed rehmannia root into the pot , simmer them with water, and screen the liquid with a piece of gauze;

2. 将大米煮半熟沥干，和药汁混匀蒸熟，再拌适量酒曲装入瓦坛中，四周用棉花或稻草保温发酵，直发到味甜即成。

2. Cook rice half done, mix it with the liquid, steam it, mix proper portion of distiller's yeast, and put them into the earthen jar. Wrap the jar with cotton or straw to keep it warm until it's sweet;

3. 每天二次，每次三汤匙，用开水冲服。

3. Take chrysanthemum wine twice a day and each time three spoons mixed with boiled water.

丛书后记

　　上下五千年的悠久历史孕育了灿烂辉煌的中华文化。我国地域辽阔,民族众多,节庆活动丰富多彩,而如此众多的节庆活动就是一座座珍贵丰富的旅游资源宝藏。在中华民族漫长的历史长河中,春节、清明、端午、中秋等传统节日和少数民族节日,是中华民族优秀传统文化的历史积淀,是中华民族精神和情感传承的重要载体,是维系祖国统一、民族团结、文化认同、社会和谐的精神纽带,是中华民族生生不息的不竭动力。

　　春节以正月为岁首,贴门神、朝贺礼;元宵节张灯、观灯;清明节扫墓、踏青、郊游、赏牡丹;端午节赛龙舟、包粽子;上巳节被禊;七夕节乞巧,牛郎会织女;中秋节赏月、食月饼;节日间的皮影戏、长安鼓乐;少数民族的节日赶圩、歌舞美食……这一桩桩有趣的节日习俗,是联络华人、华侨亲情、乡情、民族情的纽带,是中国非物质文化遗产的"活化石"。

　　为了传播中华民族优秀传统文化,推进中外文化交流,中国人类学民族学研究会民族节庆专业委员会与安徽人民出版社合作,继成功出版《中国节庆文化》丛书之后,再次推出《多彩中国节》丛书。为此,民族节庆专委会专门成立了编纂委员会,邀请了国际节庆协会(IFEA)主席兼首席执行官史蒂文·施迈德先生、中国文联原执行副主席冯骥才先生、第十一届全国政协民族和宗教委员会副主任周明甫先生等担任顾问,由《中外节庆网》总编辑彭新良博士担任主编,16 位知名学者组成编委会,负责丛书的组织策划、选题确定、体例拟定和作者的甄选。

出版《多彩中国节》丛书，是民族节庆专业委员会和安徽人民出版社合作的结晶。安徽人民出版社是安徽省最早的出版社，有60余年的建社历史，在对外传播方面走在全国出版社的前列；民族节庆专业委员会是我国节庆研究领域唯一的国家级社团，拥有丰富的专家资源和地方节庆资源。这套丛书的出版，实现了双方优势资源的整合。丛书的面世，若能对推动中国文化的对外传播、促进传统民族文化的传承与保护、展示中华民族的文化魅力、塑造节庆的品牌与形象有所裨益，我们将甚感欣慰。

掩卷沉思，这套丛书凝聚着诸位作者的智慧，倾注着编纂者的心血，也诠释着中华民族文化的灿烂与辉煌。在此，真诚感谢各位编委会成员、丛书作者、译者以及出版社工作人员付出的辛劳，以及各界朋友对丛书编纂工作的鼎力支持！希望各位读者对丛书多提宝贵意见，以便我们进一步完善后续作品，将更加璀璨的节庆文化呈现在世界面前。

为了向中外读者更加形象地展示各民族的节庆文化，本丛书选用了大量图片。这些图片，既有来自于丛书作者的亲自拍摄，也有的来自于民族节庆专委会图片库（由各地方节庆组织、节庆主办单位报送并授权使用），还有部分图片是由编委会从专业图片库购买，或从新闻媒体中转载。由于时间关系，无法与原作者一一取得联系，请有关作者与本书编委会联系（邮箱：pxl@jieqing365.com），我们将按相关规定支付稿酬。特此致谢。

《多彩中国节》丛书编委会

2018 年 3 月

Series Postscript

China has developed its splendid and profound culture during its long history of 5000 years. It has a vast territory, numerous nationalities as well as the colorful festivals. The rich festival activities have become the invaluable tourism resources. The traditional festivals, such as the Spring Festival, the Tomb-Sweeping Festival, the Dragon Boat Festival, the Mid-Autumn Festival as well as the festivals of ethnic minorities, represent the excellent traditional culture of China and have become an important carrier bearing the spirits and emotions of Chinese people, a spirit tie for the national reunification, national unity, cultural identity and social harmony, and an inexhaustible motive force for the development of Chinese nation.

The Spring Festival starts with Chinese lunar January, when people post pictures of the Door Gods and exchange gifts and wishes cheerfully. At the Lantern Festival a splendid light show is to be held and enjoyed. On the Tomb-Sweeping Festival, men and women will worship their ancestors by sweeping the tombs, going for a walk in the country and watching the peony. And then the Dragon Boat Festival witnesses a wonderful boat race and the making of zongzi. Equally interesting is the needling celebration on the Double Seventh Festival related to a touching love story of a cowboy and his fairy bride. While the Mid-Autumn Festival is characterized by moon-cake eating and moon watching. Besides all these, people can also enjoy shadow puppet shows, Chang'an drum performance, along with celebration fairs, songs and dances and delicious snacks for ethic groups. A variety of festival entertainment and celebrations have formed a bond among all Chinese, at home or abroad, and they are regarded as the "living fossil" of Chinese intangible cultural heritage.

In order to spread the excellent traditional culture of China, and promote the folk festival brand for our country, the Folk Festival Commission of the China Union of Anthropological and Ethnological Science (CUAES) has worked with the Anhui People's Publishing House to publish *The Colorful Chinese Festivals Series*. For this purpose, the Folk Festival Commission has established the editorial board of *The Colorful Chinese Festivals Series*, by inviting Mr. Steven Wood Schmader, president and CEO of the International Festival And Events Association (IFEA); Mr. Feng Jicai, former executive vice-president of China Federation of Literary and Art Circles(CFLAC); Mr. Zhou Mingfu, deputy director of the Eleventh National and Religious Committee of the CPPCC as consultants; Dr. Peng Xinliang, editor-in-chief of the Chinese and foreign Festival Website as the chief editor; and 16 famous scholars as the members to organize, plan, select and determine the topics and the authors.

This series is the product of the cooperation between the Folk Festival Commission and Anhui People's Publishing House. Anhui People's Publishing House is the first publishing house in Anhui Province, which has a history of over 60 years, and has been in the leading position in terms of foreign transmission. The Folk Festival Commission is the only organization of national level in the field of research of the Chinese festivals, which has experts and rich local festival resources. The series has integrated the advantageous resources of both parties. We will be delighted and gratified to see that the series could promote the foreign transmission of the Chinese culture, promote the inheritance and preservation of the traditional and folk cultures, express the cultural charms of China and build the festival brand and image of China.

The Colorful Chinese Festivals Series is bearing the wisdoms and knowledge of all of its authors and the great efforts of the editors, and explaining the splendid cultures of the Chinese nation. We hereby sincerely express our gratitude to the members of the board, the authors, the translators and the personnel in the publishing house for their great efforts and to all friends from all walks of the society for their supports. We hope you can provide your invaluable opinions for us to further promote the following works so as to show the world our excellent festival culture.

This series uses a large number of pictures in order to unfold the festive cultures in a vivid way to readers at home and abroad. Some of them are shot by the authors themselves, some of them come from the picture database of the Folk Festival Commission (contributed and authorized by the local folk festival organizations or organizers of local festival celebrations), and some of them are bought from Saitu Website or taken from the news media. Because of the limit of time, we can't contact the contributors one by one. Please don't hesitate about contacting the editorial board of this series (e-mail: pxl@jieqing365.com) if you're the contributor. We'll pay you by conforming to the state stipulations.

Editorial Committee of *The Colorful Chinese Festivals Series*
March, 2018